The New
CAMBRIDGE
English Course

PRACTICE

2

MICHAEL SWAN
CATHERINE WALTER

CAMBRIDGE
UNIVERSITY PRESS

PUBLISHED BY THE PRESS SYNDICATE OF THE UNIVERSITY OF CAMBRIDGE
The Pitt Building, Trumpington Street, Cambridge, United Kingdom

CAMBRIDGE UNIVERSITY PRESS
The Edinburgh Building, Cambridge CB2 2RU, UK   http://www.cup.cam.ac.uk
40 West 20th Street, New York, NY 10011–4211, USA   http://www.cup.org
10 Stamford Road, Oakleigh, Melbourne 3166, Australia

First published 1990
Fifteenth printing 1999

Printed in the United Kingdom at the University Press, Cambridge

The texts and exercises in the *Additional reading* section
on pages 108 to 114 were compiled by Christine Lindop
and Dominic Fisher.

ISBN 0 521 37650 5 Practice Book 2

Practice Book 2 split edition:
ISBN 0 521 37655 6 Practice Book 2A
ISBN 0 521 37656 4 Practice Book 2B

ISBN 0 521 37662 9 Practice Book 2 with Key

ISBN 0 521 37638 6 Student's Book 2

Student's Book 2 split edition:
ISBN 0 521 37643 2 Student's Book 2A
ISBN 0 521 37644 0 Student's Book 2B

ISBN 0 521 37666 1 Teacher's Book 2

ISBN 0 521 37670 X Test Book 2

ISBN 0 521 37503 7 Class Cassette Set 2

ISBN 0 521 37507 X Student's Cassette Set 2

Student's Cassettes 2 split edition:
ISBN 0 521 38224 6 Student's Cassette 2A
ISBN 0 521 38225 4 Student's Cassette 2B
ISBN 0 521 45934 6 Video 2 (VHS PAL)
ISBN 0 521 45936 2 Video 2 (VHS SECAM)
ISBN 0 521 45935 4 Video 2 (VHS NTSC)
ISBN 0 521 45939 7 Video Teacher's Guide 2 with photocopiable tasks
ISBN 0 521 45940 0 Video Teacher's Guide 2
ISBN 0 521 45941 9 Video Student Activity Book 2

Contents

1 May I introduce myself?

1 Fill in the gaps in the conversations.

TOM: Jake, 1 _'d_ like to 2 _introduce_ my friend Alice.
ALICE: How 3 _do you do_?
JAKE: How 4 _do you do_?

ANN: Andy, 5 _this_ is Louise.
ANDY: Hello, Louise. I'm 6 _glad_ to 7 _meet_ you.

JOE: Hello, Phil. How 8 _are you_?
PHIL: Fine, 9 _thanks_, Joe. I'm 10 _glad_ to see you again.

CATHY: Janet, 11 _do you know_ Susan?
JANET: No. How do you do? I've heard 12 _so_ much 13 _about_ you.

JUDY: 14 _May_ I introduce 15 _myself_? My 16 _name's_ Judy Gower.
RUTH: Hello. I'm Ruth Collins. I'm sorry, I didn't 17 _catch_ your name.

KATE: Where are you from?
MARK: Canada.
KATE: 18 _Whereabouts_ in Canada?
MARK: Toronto.

STEVE: 19 _Excuse_ me. 20 _Aren't_ you Liz Bush?
LIZ: Yes, that's 21 _right_.

2 Match the questions and the answers.

1. What nationality are you? – c
2. What sports do you do? – k
3. What kind of music do you like? – i
4. What kind of books do you read? – b
5. Are you shy? – f
6. Can you play the piano? – n
7. What do you like doing in your spare time? – a
8. Why are you learning English? – l
9. Where do you live? – e
10. Do you like watching football matches? – h
11. What does your father look like? – j
12. What's your mother like? – d
13. Have you got any sisters or brothers? – m
14. How do you feel about snakes? – g   змии

a. Knitting and reading.
b. Mostly novels; sometimes history books.
c. Austrian.
d. She's very calm and cheerful.   весел
e. In a small town near Vienna.
f. No, I'm fairly self-confident.   доста уверен
g. They don't interest me.
h. I prefer playing games to watching them.
i. Classical music.
j. He's tall and fair.
k. Long-distance running.
l. I'd like to travel more, and I think it's a useful language.
m. Yes, two sisters.
n. Yes, but not very well.

3 Here are some answers. What are the questions?

1. Carlos Peña. _What is your name?_
2. Venezuela. _Where are you from?_
3. I'm an engineer. _What do you do?_
4. 25. _How old are you?_
5. One metre seventy-eight. _How tall are you?_
6. Two brothers and a sister. _Have you got any_
7. No, I'm not.
8. In a small flat in Caracas. _Whereabouts in Caracas_
9. I need to read it for my work.
10. No, but I can speak a little French.
11. I watch TV or I go out with friends. _What do you do in your spare time?_
12. No, I don't, but I like dancing.
13. About twice a week. _How often you play tennis_

4 Vocabulary revision. Complete the lists and answer the questions.

1. Monday, Tu_____, W_____, _____, _____, _____, _____.
2. January, Feb_____, M_____, _____, _____, _____, _____, _____, _____, _____, _____, _____.
3. What day(s) do you have English lessons?
4. What day(s) do you NOT go to any classes?
5. What day is/was your birthday this year?
6. What month is your birthday?
7. What month is your father's birthday?   _in June_
8. What month is your mother's birthday?
9. What is the coldest month in your country?
10. What is the hottest month in your country?

except – измирене

5 If you have Student's Cassette A, find Lesson 1, Exercise 1. Listen and repeat. Try for good intonation.

From Monday true Saturday

6 Read this. The first time you read it, don't look up more than ten words in the dictionary.

A: People who are learning to be family therapists do this exercise very early in their course. They're put together in a room and asked to choose another person from the group who makes them think of someone in their family; or who they think could belong in their family. And – here's the interesting bit – they're not allowed to talk at all while they're choosing. They just stand up and walk around looking at all the others. When everybody has chosen somebody, they talk together for a time, to see if they can find out if their families are similar. Then each pair, without talking, chooses another pair, to make groups of four. Then they talk together about what it was in their family backgrounds that led to their decisions. And finally, they report to all the others what they've discovered.

B: Which is?

A: That they've all, somehow, picked out three people whose families functioned in very similar ways to their own.

B: What do you mean, 'functioned in very similar ways'?

A: Well, all four come from families where there was difficulty in sharing affection; or perhaps in expressing anger; or where everyone was expected always to be optimistic and cheerful. Or they might find out that all four of them were from families where the father was away from home a lot of the time; or that they all suffered some sort of important loss or change at about the same age. And this tells us something about why people fall in love with one another!

(Adapted from *Families and how to survive them* by Robin Skynner and John Cleese)

2 Who's who?

1 Put the right words with the different parts of the body. Use your dictionary to find out more words for parts of the body if you want to.

arm	beard	chest	ear	eye	face
finger	foot	hair	hand	head	knee
leg	mouth	neck	nose	shoulder	
stomach					

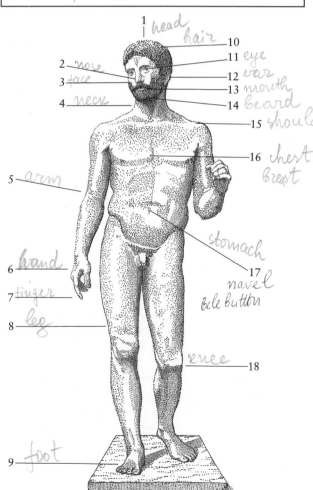

1 head
2 nose
3 face
4 neck
5 arm
6 hand
7 finger
8 leg
9 foot
10 hair
11 eye
12 ear
13 mouth
14 beard
15 shoulder
16 chest / breast
17 stomach / navel / belle button
18 knee

2 Read the advertisement with a dictionary, copy some of the questions and write true answers.
Example:

Are you young and fit?   Yes, I am.

Are you young and fit? Are you interested in people? Have you got a nice voice? Can you speak two or more languages? Can you swim? Have you got your own car? Can you go for a long time without sleep? Are you patient with children? Are you good at maths? Can you play a musical instrument? If you can answer yes to all these questions, write to Box 4762 for details of a wonderful job opportunity.

3 Make questions as in the examples.

Those houses are expensive. (*big*)
Are those houses big?

All the family can speak French. (*Spanish*)
Can all the family speak Spanish?

Alice has got a dog. (*horse*)
Has Alice got a horse?

1. Her little girl can sing. (*dance*)
2. The room is comfortable. (*expensive*)
3. The police have got his description. (*name*)
4. The film is very interesting. (*long*)
5. His sister has got blue eyes. (*fair hair*)
6. Everybody has got something to drink. (*eat*)
7. Sally can play the piano. (*guitar*)
8. The lessons are useful. (*interesting*)
9. Jake can swim very fast. (*run*)
10. Her new boyfriend is very nice. (*intelligent*)

7

matchmaker – сватовщи-
ца

4 Have you got everything you want? No? What haven't you got? Write some sentences. Examples:

I haven't got a raincoat.   *I haven't got any English friends.*
I haven't got many nice clothes.   *I haven't got enough books.*

наличу
свободного

5 As quickly as you can, look through the texts and match the descriptions with the pictures on page 10 of the Student's Book. Time limit: 3 minutes.

1 the police are looking for a man of about 20, of average height, with short fair hair, green eyes and a large nose. When last seen, he was wearing a blue sweater and grey

Rob

Address: 43 Park End Road, Leamington.

Date and place of birth: 21.6.1970, London.

Present age: 20

Height: 1m 62

Weight: 58kg

Colour of hair: dark brown

Colour of eyes: brown

2 Education:

3 *Sally*

Although we haven't met yet, I feel we're friends already.
It's so kind of you to offer to meet me at the station on the 12.45 train from Coventry. I haven't got a photo to send you, but I'm easy to recognise – I'm very tall and thin, I've got dark hair and brown eyes, and I wear big glasses. I'm looking forward very much to meeting you.

Yours,

Jake

Can you speak two or more languages? Are you a good listener? Do you like music, theatre and walking? If so, perhaps you are the woman for me. Good-looking, intelligent, interesting man, young 45, seeks beautiful cultured woman for serious relationship. Write Box 363, *Daily News.*

5

4 *C*

very pretty, with long fair hair and a big warm smile. It's funny, she thinks her nose is too big, but I think it's just right. She's got a great sense of humour, she's full of life and she can dance all night. I think

Anna

January last year. At 43, she is the youngest Minister in the new government. Educated at Rumbold Comprehensive and Leeds University, she entered politics in her twenties and became a Member of Parliament at 28. She is married, and has three children. Her husband is a local government officer, and

6

6 If you have Student's Cassette A, find Lesson 2, Exercise 1. Listen to the recording and try to write down everything Polly says.

8

3 My mornings usually start fairly late

1 Write the correct forms of the verbs.

1. My father always _makes_ Sunday dinner. (*make*)
2. Ruth _doesn't eat_ eggs; they _make_ her ill. (*not eat; make*)
3. 'Have you got a light, by any chance?' 'Sorry, I _don't smoke_ (*smoke*)
4. Where _does_ Mark _go_ to school? (*go*)
5. _Do_ your parents _like_ your girlfriend? (*like*)
6. How often _do_ you _go_ swimming? (*go*)
7. Where _does_ your sister _work_? (*work*)
8. Ann _doesn't_ usually _have_ lunch. (*not have*)
9. Who _does_ the ironing in your house? (*do*)
10. We _don't go_ out during the week. (*not go*)
11. My uncle _worries_ a lot. (*worry*)
12. Veronica _watches_ *Mastermind* every week. (*watch*)

2 Rewrite the sentences, adding the frequency adverbs.

1. I get up quite early on Saturdays. (*usually*)
2. My son goes to school on Saturday morning. (*normally*)
3. My daughter goes to a gym club. (*quite often*)
4. After gym club, we go to the bakery for fresh cakes. (*almost always*)
5. In the afternoon, the children's father takes them somewhere like a museum or a zoo. (*often*)
6. We try to go away and visit friends. (*once a month*)
7. On Sundays, I get up before ten. (*hardly ever*)
8. I go to church, but my husband does. (*never; sometimes*)
9. We have guests for Sunday lunch. (*quite often*)
10. We visit my father and mother. (*every week*)

3 Look at the two pictures. How often do you think they do the things in the box? Examples:

Chris tidies her room once every six months.
Lucy brushes her teeth three times a day.

Chris   Lucy

wash hair	tidy room	go to hairdresser's
empty wastepaper basket		change socks
have bath	change bed	brush teeth

4 Read the text without using a dictionary, and try to match the pictures and the words. Then you can use your dictionary if you want.

His name is Mani Lal. Like his father and his grandfathers in central Nepal, he is a honey hunter. With only a rope round his waist, he hangs over a 120-metre cliff on a rope ladder to harvest the sweet treasure of *Apis laboriosa*, the world's largest honeybee.

Thousands of angry bees fill the air as he pushes a bamboo pole into their nest. But over his everyday shirt he wears only a loose cape on his head and a pair of old trousers given to him by a cousin serving in the British army.

Using his poles like enormous Japanese chopsticks, he cuts thick pieces of honeycomb into a bamboo basket lined with the skin of a wild goat. When the basket is full, he lowers it to his friends at the bottom of the cliff.

The sound of the giant bees is frightening, but Mani Lal moves quickly and calmly. He has done this many times. He is 64 years old.

(from an article by E. Valli and D. Summers, *National Geographic* magazine)

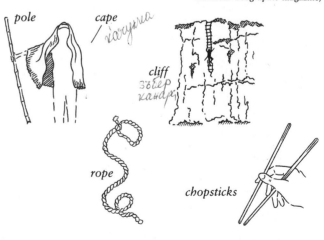

pole   cape

cliff

rope

chopsticks

5 How do you spend your weekend? Write 100 words or more.

6 If you have Student's Cassette A, find Lesson 3, Exercise 1 (only part of Rufus's monologue is recorded here). Listen, and try to write everything down.

4 How people live

1 Make at least six sentences.

| In Italy
In Britain
In China
etc. | people often eat
people often drink | tea
rice
spaghetti
etc. |

2 Change these sentences as in the examples.

She doesn't like hot weather. (*cold*)
———→*She likes cold weather.*

They eat fish. (*X meat*)
———→*They don't eat meat.*

He works on Saturdays. (*? Sundays*)
———→*Does he work on Sundays?*

1. He lives in a tent. (*X house*)
2. They work at home. (*X office*)
3. It always rains there in winter. (*? summer*)
4. She doesn't speak Chinese. (*Japanese*)
5. We like Ann and Peter. (*X their children*)
6. You play football. (*? tennis*)
7. He often travels to America. (*X Africa*)
8. He doesn't eat in restaurants. (*at home*)
9. He cooks for himself. (*X other people*)
10. She knows how to make friends.
    (*X make money*)
11. She doesn't like pop music.
    (*classical music*)
12. He reads a lot. (*? novels*)
13. The train runs on Mondays and Wednesdays.
    (*? Fridays*)
14. The price doesn't include service. (*tax*)
15. Our cat eats meat. (*X fish*)

3 Practise saying these words with the correct stress.

| desert | Australia | Brazil | climate | January |
| village | around | vegetable | animal | difficult |

4 Write a few sentences for an Amazon Indian or an Australian aborigine, to tell him/her how you live.

5 Read this, using a dictionary where necessary.

GYPSIES

Around the year 1000 AD, some people from north-west India began to travel westwards – nobody knows why. After leaving their homes, they did not settle down again, but spent their lives moving from one place to another.

Their descendants are called the Romany people, or Gypsies. There are Gypsies all over the world, and many of them are still travelling, with no fixed homes. There are about eight million of them, including three million in eastern Europe.

Gypsies sometimes have a hard time in the countries where they travel. Because they are different, people may be afraid of them, look down on them, or think that they are criminals. The Nazis persecuted the Gypsies, like the Jews, and nobody knows how many of them died in Hitler's death camps.

Gypsies have their own language, Romany. They like music and dancing, and they often work in fairs and circuses. Travelling is very important to them, and many Gypsies are unhappy if they have to stay in one place. Because of this, it is difficult for Gypsy children to go to school, and Gypsies are often illiterate. In some places, the education authorities try to arrange special travelling schools for Gypsy children, so that they can get the same education as other children.

"Well, seeing as you ask, this is the National Costume of Uranus."

5 There's a strange light in the sky

1 Read the commentary and decide where to put the verbs from the box.

. . . and Mrs Rask's car ......1...... in front of the palace. This is a historic moment – as I am sure you know, she is the first Fantasian president to visit our country since 1954. President and Mrs Martin ......2...... down the steps to welcome her. And now the car has stopped, and Mrs Rask ......3...... out. There seems to be some problem with the door. No, it's all right. President Martin and Mrs Rask ......4...... hands – and the crowds ......5...... crazy – people ......6...... and shouting. What an occasion this is! And now Mrs Martin ......7...... to the Fantasian president. I expect she ......8...... if she had a good journey. The Fantasian president ......9...... Mrs Martin – I don't know what she ......10....., but I think she ......11...... a joke – everybody's laughing. Now President Martin ......12...... the Foreign Minister and his staff to our distinguished visitor. I must say that Mrs Rask ......13...... *beautiful* – she ......14...... Fantasian national costume: a long green and gold silk dress with a lovely pattern of flowers, and a tall red hat. President and Mrs Martin are dressed very simply, as usual: he's wearing a dark blue suit with a light blue shirt and black tie, and Mrs Martin is wearing a brown tweed skirt with a white blouse and light brown shoes. What an experience this is! What a historic moment! And now they're ......15...... and going inside the palace. The President is leading the way . . .

are cheering	are coming	are going
are shaking	're turning	is answering
's asking	is getting	is introducing
is looking	's making	's saying
is stopping	is talking	's wearing

2 Imagine that an important person is visiting your home town or your school. Write a short commentary (like the text in Exercise 1).

3 Make questions. Be careful of the word order. Example:

Where | the President and his wife | standing
——→ *Where are the President and his wife standing?*
(NOT *Where are standing the President . . . ?*)

1. What | Mrs Andrews | writing
2. What | that girl | eating
3. Why | those old men | singing
4. Why | the car | making a funny noise
5. What | Mrs Harris | trying to say
6. Where | your aunt | working just now
7. Dr Parker | working | today
8. your TV | working all right

4 Write some sentences to say what you are *not* doing at this moment.

5 Do you know the names of all these articles of clothing? Use your dictionary to help you.

6 If you have Student's Cassette A, find Lesson 5, Exercise 1. Listen to the recording and write down five or more phrases or sentences that give different information from the pictures in Student's Book Exercise 1. Example:

with the score at Spain 8, England 1

6 Things are changing

1 How are you changing?

(Are you getting fatter / thinner / taller / richer / poorer / better at English / more tired / happier / unhappier / more beautiful / more handsome / more intelligent / . . . ?)

2 Complete the sentences with some of these words and expressions.

are getting	are going	army	average
changing	fast	height	is getting
is happening	price	problem	slowly
unemployed	worse		

1. The *price* of petrol is going up again.
2. Three years ago there were two million people without jobs. Now there are over three million *unemployed*
3. The housing problem is getting *worse*
4. Food prices *are going* up.
5. Things are changing very *fast* these days.
6. Restaurants *are getting* more and more expensive.
7. In 1981, the *average* cost of a good meal for two, with wine, was £25.
8. There are 300,000 men in the *army*
9. What *is happening*? I can't see.

3 Make questions with *getting* or *going* about these things:

1. the price of drinking water
   Why is the price of drinking water going up?
2. inflation
   How fast is inflation going down?
3. my mother's cold
   Is your mother's cold getting better?
4. the number of university students *going up*
5. my sister's husband *getting happier*
6. the baby's weight *going up*
7. Sunday newspapers *getting funny*
8. the number of road accidents
9. the price of air tickets
10. the Atlantic Ocean

4 Which one is different? Why? Example:

milk   tomato   steak   chair   wine
Chair – not food or drink

1. milk   wine   water   juice   (apple)
2. chair   TV   fridge   (bus)   sofa
3. chair   (TV)   fridge   sofa   armchair
4. tall   (intelligent)   fair   handsome
5. divorced   married   single   (happy)
6. April   February   (Thursday)   September
7. Africa   America   (Japan)   Europe   Asia
8. (airport)   kitchen   bathroom   bedroom

5 Read this with a dictionary.

WE ARE GETTING HAPPIER

People are getting happier. According to a recent report from the Western Statistics Office, 73% of people say that they are happy 'most of the time', compared with only 47% at the beginning of the century. Perhaps this is partly because the world is less crowded: the Western population is going down by about 1.3% per year. And life expectancy is increasing: in 1970, men lived for an average of 69 years and women 75; both sexes now can expect to live for 113 years. We are getting richer, too. The average income in 2096 was 146,000 Western Credits – twice as much as in the year 2018.

The biochemical revolution is nearly complete: 94% of the population is now green. (For some reason only 83% have green hair, but scientists expect to solve the last remaining problems by the year 2100.)

Not everything is getting better, though. The climate is still changing for the worse, and sea levels are continuing to rise. If average temperatures go on increasing, scientists are afraid that more of the world's capitals will go the same way as London, Paris and New York. Perhaps one day we will all have to move to the mountains.

Religious belief is becoming much less common. In 2018, 65% of Western Federation citizens said that they believed in God; in 2096 the figure was only 24%, and only half of these went to church regularly.

(Figures from the WSO Annual Report, July 2098)

(From *The Times*, 18 July 2098)

6 Write a similar report from *The Times* for 18 July 2198.

Summary A

1 Write these numbers in words.

1st   2nd   3rd   4th   5th   6th   8th
9th   12th   20th   100th

2 Write the contractions.

is not *isn't*

was not   I have   she has   she is   I would
you are   do not   does not   cannot   I will

12

3 Write the third-person singular forms.

stop *stops*   start *starts*

see   like   work   catch   lie   finish   pass   hurry   send   go

4 Here are pieces of some pictures. What do you think the woman is doing in each one?

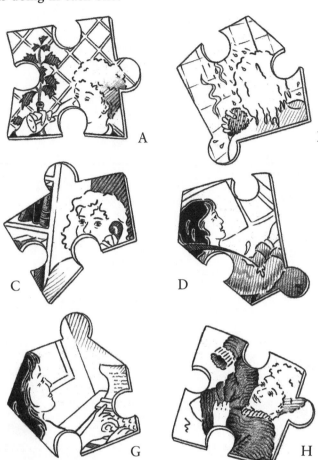

A. She is drinking a glass of wine.

B. ....

A   B   C   D   E   F   G   H   I   J

5 Complete the text with the words and expressions from the box.

My first real ___1___ *girlfriend* was a very ___2___ *beautiful* girl called Penny. She was ___3___ tall, ___4___ slim ___5___ fat, with a lovely figure. She had ___6___, ___7___ *fair* hair and ___8___ *blue* eyes, a funny short ___9___ *nose*, and a wide mouth with a wonderful ___10___ *smile*, like the sun coming out. Her voice was soft and nice to ___11___ *listen* to. She had a great sense of humour, and we ___12___ *laughed* a lot. At nights she ___13___ *worked* as a nurse in a mental hospital, and she was often very ___14___ *tired* when we saw ___15___, but she was ___16___ fun to be with. She was a very talented actress, and I will never ___17___ her playing Hermione in a student production of ___18___ *Shakespeare's Winter's Tale*. Penny was a lovely ___19___, and I was lucky to know ___20___. I often wonder what she ___21___ *is doing* now.

6 Write a description of yourself or of somebody you like. Use some words and expressions from Exercise 5.

I'm tall and fair, with blue eyes and a small nose.
My feet are quite big, but I think I'm quite nice-looking.
I like dancing and listening to music.

wonder

Revision A

1 Is or has?

1. She's 37.
2. It's late.
3. He's 1m 85cm tall.
4. What's he done?
5. She's got blue eyes.
6. He's wearing a dark suit.
7. She's hungry.
8. He's cold.
9. He's married.
10. What colour's your new car?
11. She's gone to London.
12. She's tired.

2 Put in one of these words.

somebody	anybody	everybody	nobody
something	anything	everything	nothing
somewhere	anywhere	everywhere	nowhere

1. *Nobody* can speak all the languages in the world.
2. I think there's *somebody* at the door.
3. 'Where are my keys?' 'I've seen them *somewhere*, but I can't remember where.'
4. Have you got *anything* to eat?
5. Does *anybody* know where I put my glasses?
6. You can find Coca-Cola *everywhere*.
7. I need *something* to read – have you got a paper?
8. I'm bored – there's *nothing* to do.
9. *Everybody* needs love.
10. He and his wife always tell each other *everything*.
11. 'Come and see a film with us.' 'I don't want to go *anywhere*.'
12. 'Where can I find a good job with plenty of money and no work?' '*Nowhere*.'
13. 'Mary's here.' 'I don't want to see *anybody*.'
14. They're a very loving couple. They go *everywhere* together.
15. 'Do you know Sid?' 'Yes, *everybody* knows Sid.'
16. 'Is *everything* all right?' 'Yes, thanks – no problems.'
17. I can't find my coat *anywhere*.
18. 'Did *anybody* telephone yesterday?' 'No, *nobody*.'
19. I can't understand *anything* she says – not a word.
20. 'What would you like?' '*Nothing* just now, thank you.'

3 Put in the correct verb forms.

1. Look! It *'s raining* again. (*rain*)
2. It always *rains* when I want to go for a walk. (*rain*)
3. 'What *are* you *doing*?' 'I'm *writing* a letter.' (*do; write*)
4. 'What *do* you *do*?' 'I'm an electrical engineer.' (*do*)
5. '*Do* you *like* fish?' 'Not very much.' (*like*)
6. 'Have you got a cigarette?' 'Sorry, I *don't smoke*.' (*not smoke*)
7. 'What time *do* you *get* up?' 'At seven o'clock, usually.' (*get*)
8. 'Would you like to play tennis tomorrow?' 'Sorry, I'm *playing* with Bill.' (*play*)
9. I *work* most Saturday mornings. (*work*)
10. 'Is your father here?' 'No, he's *shopping*.' (*shop*)

4 If you have Student's Cassette A, find Revision Lesson A, Listening Exercise 2. Listen to the story and decide whether these sentences are true or false.

1. You're walking along a beach. (*True*)
2. It's a cold day. (*False*)
3. You're walking quite fast.
4. You sit down on the sand.
5. You throw four stones into the water.
6. You walk into the water.
7. An old man walks out of the sea.
8. He's got beautiful long hair.
9. You close your eyes for a few minutes.
10. You see him walking away.
11. You go to a large house.
12. When you wake up you see the man again.

"That funny noise is getting louder."

plenty – изобилие

give up < передавать ся
отказываться ся

14

5 Read the text. Use a dictionary if it is really necessary. Then decide which picture shows the woman's dream.

(This is from a science fiction story. A woman who lives on a distant planet, millions of miles away from the earth, is talking to her husband.)

"I dreamed about a man."

"A man?"

"A tall man, six feet one inch tall."

"How absurd; a giant, a misshapen giant."

"Somehow" – she tried the words – "he looked all right. In spite of being tall. And he had – oh, I know you'll think it silly – he had *blue* eyes!"

"Blue eyes! Gods!" cried Mr K. "What'll you dream next? I suppose he had *black* hair?"

"How did you *guess*?" She was excited.

"I picked the most unlikely colour," he replied coldly.

"Well, black it was!" she cried. "And he had a very white skin; oh, he was *most* unusual! He was dressed in a strange uniform and he came down out of the sky and spoke pleasantly to me." She smiled.

"Out of the sky; what nonsense!"

"He came in a metal thing that glittered in the sun," she remembered. She closed her eyes to shape it again. "I dreamed there was the sky and something sparkled like a coin thrown in the air, and suddenly it grew large and fell down softly to land, a long silver craft, round and alien. And a door opened in the side of the silver object and this tall man stepped out. He looked at me and he said 'I've come from the third planet in my ship. My name is Nathaniel York –'"

"A stupid name; it's no name at all," objected the husband.

"Of course it's stupid, because it's a dream," she explained softly. "And he said, 'This is the first trip across space. There are only two of us in our ship, myself and my friend Bert.'"

"*Another* stupid name."

"And he said, 'We're from a city on *Earth*; that's the name of our planet,'" continued Mrs K. "That's what he said."

Mr K turned away. She stopped him with a word. "Yll?" she called quietly. "Do you ever wonder if – well, if there *are* people living on the third planet?"

(from *The Martian Chronicles* by Ray Bradbury)

A

B

C

6 Try the crossword.

(crossword grid with answers partially filled in)

ACROSS

1. May I .... myself? My name's Sue Carter.
5. Her hair is the same colour .... mine.
9. Dogs, horses, tigers and elephants are all ....s.
10. Not long.
11. Sally and Phil love .... other very much.
14. 1.6 kilometres.
15. Would you like ...to... dance?
19. The strange creature's holding a ...gun... and pointing it at me.
20. How do you .... this word?
22. You and I.
24. Hello.
26. That man.
27. Goodbye.
29. Perhaps.
30. The opposite of *white*.
32. I usually work .... home.
34. 'It's getting very late.' '................. what?'
36. The same as *26 across*.
37. Not square.
39. Negative answer.
42. A bad thing to happen when you're driving.
45. What's the .... between *strange* and *foreign*?
46. 'I hate golf.' '................. do I.'
47. Not wet.

DOWN

1. Not outside.
2. She's very pretty. Her eyes are a bit small, ...
3. How .... do you travel by air?
4. Without a job.
5. He's .... architect.
6. Please .... down.
7. A kind of *9 across*.
8. What's he like, ...?
9. 'Nice to see you again, John.' '................., my name's Peter.'
12. by .... = by plane.
13. coat, trousers, blouse, pants, shirt, *etc.*
16. Are you doing anything .... Tuesday?
17. Excuse ....
18. All the people.
21. I'm sorry. I didn't .... your name.
23. 'How did you get here?' '................. train.'
25. I am.
27. A kind of food.
28. You've got one on each side of your head.
31. You can open things with this.
33. 'What's the time?' 'Twenty .... three.'
35. 'How often do you see Harry?' 'About .... a week.'

38. You can .... a dictionary if necessary.
40. Would you like tea .... coffee?
41. We live .... a small flat on the third floor.
43. The same .... *5 across*.
44. *34 across* is the same as *46 across*, and .... is *44 down*.

(*Solution on page 116.*)

"Poor Fred, we just stopped to take a photograph, and it was love at first sight."

16

7 A true story

1 Read the text and fill in the gaps with words from the two lists.

(There have been many reports of 'UFOs' – unidentified flying objects – over the last few years. Many people believe that these UFOs come from other worlds, far away in space. Here is one report from an American newspaper.)

On June 14th, in Carmel, Indiana, a woman _saw_ a large strange bright light moving around in the sky. The woman, Mrs Dora Gabb, 34, _phoned_ ¹ the police _and_ ² _spoke_ to Patrolman Conrad Brown, _who_ ² _came_ straight to her house to investigate. _When_ ² he arrived there was nothing to be seen, _but_ ² ten minutes later Mrs Gabb's 14-year-old daughter Leslie _ran_ into the house screaming. Leslie _said_ ²and she and a girlfriend were riding on motor-bicycles in the woods _when_ they _saw_ 'a large object, bigger than a house' directly in front of them, low in the sky. It _had_ a green top, white sides, a reddish purple tail, and lights of purple, green, gold, red and blue. It _made_ no sound. The girls' bicycles _stop_ working, _and_ the girls '_felt_ strange'. The spaceship _came_ down lower, _and_ _stayed_ for some time about 100 feet above the ground, not moving. _then_, with a whistling sound, it _left_ at high speed.

LIST 1

Put the past tenses of these verbs into the gaps marked '1'.

come   come   feel   have
leave   make   phone   run
see   see   say   speak
stay   stop

LIST 2

Put these words into the gaps marked '2'.

and   and   and   but
that   then   when   when
who

"I knew she was going out with a coloured chap, but never thought it was green."

" . . . and the next contestant hoping to become Miss Universe . . ."

2 This is part of a conversation between a policeman and a young woman. Fill in the gaps. The words in the box will help you.

> arrive   do   go   make   see   stop   take   telephone
> travel   watch

POLICEMAN: What time _did you stop_ ¹ work yesterday?
WOMAN: I don't know. About half past five.
POL: And where _did you go_ ² after that?
WOM: I went straight home.
POL: I see. How _did_ ³ home? By bus?
WOM: Yes.
POL: What bus _did you take_ ⁴?
WOM: I don't remember.
POL: All right. What time _arrived_ ⁵ home?
WOM: Oh, around six, I suppose.
POL: _Did you see_ ⁶ anybody you knew on the way?

WOM: I don't think so. I don't remember.
POL: What _did you do_ ⁷ when you got home?
WOM: Made a cup of tea and put the TV on.
POL: Oh, yes. What programme _did you watch_ ⁸?
WOM: 'Front page'.
POL: 'Front page' wasn't on last night.
WOM: I've got it recorded on video.
POL: I see. _Did you make_ ⁹ any phone calls?
WOM: Pardon?
POL: _telephone_ ¹⁰ anybody?
WOM: I might have done. I don't remember.

17

[handwritten top margin: I didn't go to the mountains]

3 Write sentences with *not*.

1. Beethoven wrote symphonies. (*books*)
   Beethoven did not write books.
2. I went to the seaside last weekend. (*the mountains*)
3. It snowed yesterday. (*rain*) *It didn't rain*
4. I enjoyed the food at the restaurant. (*the wine*)
5. I found the shoes I wanted. (*the sweater*)
6. My mother lived abroad when she was young. (*in Britain*)
7. She fell in love with an American. (*an Englishman*) *didn't fall*
8. Her parents wanted her to marry an Englishman. (*the American*)
9. She did what she wanted. (*what her parents wanted*)
   She didn't do what ...

4 Write the past tense forms of these infinitives. If you have problems, turn to page 116 in the back of the Practice Book for some rules.

1. play   start   show   watch   work
2. hate   hope   like   use
3. shop   stop
4. carry   try   worry

5 Write down five things that you did not do yesterday.

6 If you have Student's Cassette A, find Lesson 7, Exercise 5. Listen, and write down as much as you can.

---

8 I was getting ready to come home . . .

1 Read the dialogue (Student's Book Exercise 1) again. Then complete the following conversation.

ANN: Hello, darling. ......1...... [*Did you have*] a nice day?
PAT: So-so. John came in this morning, and said he ......2...... [*had*] to talk to me.
ANN: What ......3...... [*about*]?
PAT: Oh, his marriage, as ......4...... [*usual*]. We ......5...... [*had*] lunch together, and we had a long ......6...... [*talk*], and he said he felt better.
ANN: Where ......7...... [*did you*] have lunch? Somewhere ......8...... [*nice*]?
PAT: No, we went to the pub round the ......9...... [*corner*]. I just had a beer and a sandwich. Then in the afternoon Alice phoned and talked ......10...... [*for*] hours. Just ......11...... [*when*] I was trying to do some ......12...... [*more*].
ANN: I *am* sorry. It ......13...... [*sounds*] like a difficult day.
PAT: Well, it was quite interesting, but I ......14...... [*didn't*] get much work done.

2 Put in the right tense (Simple Past or Past Progressive).

1. When I *was cleaning* the house, I *found* some old letters. (*clean; find*)
2. The doorbell *rang* while I *was having* a bath. (*ring; have*)
3. We *had* an accident when we *were coming* back from holiday. (*have; come*)
4. When I looked out of the window, I *realised* that it *was raining* (*realise; rain*)
5. I *met* my wife when we *were living* in Washington. (*meet; live*)
6. I *stopped* at a garage because the car *was running* badly. (*stop; run*)
7. I suddenly *thought* of you while I *was washing up* (*think; wash up*)
8. She *went* to sleep while I *was telling* her about my holidays. (*go; tell*)
9. When I *looked* up, water *was coming* through the ceiling. (*look; come*)

realise — осознавать

3 Revision. Put in the right prepositions. (Sometimes no preposition is necessary.)

1. She works *just* nine *past* five except *on* Saturdays.
2. I was born *on* the first day of spring.
3. Can you come and stay with us *in* August?
4. What are you doing .... this evening?
5. I'm working until seven, but I'm free *after* that.
6. We're going to Morocco in May *for* three weeks.
7. Let's go walking *at* the weekend.
8. Are you free .... next Monday?
9. I'll see you *at* eight o'clock.
10. I always work better *in* the morning than *in* the afternoon.

4 Write these times in another way.

3.15 a quarter past three

4.50 ten to five

6.30   7.25   2.45   4.40
9.55   10.00   1.20   8.05

5 Copy the letter and put in correct punctuation marks and capital letters.

dear kumiko

im sorry i didnt come and see you today but things have been awful. i didnt hear my alarm clock so i got up late, then just as i was running out of the house i fell and hurt my knee. i had to go to the hospital and wait a very long time. three people who had been in a serious car crash came in while i was waiting and of course they had to go straight in before me, the doctor says nothing is broken but i mustnt stand up much for the next two or three weeks which is not very easy, this is why i am writing this note which peter is delivering for me i will let you know when i am better and perhaps you can come round for a meal.

i wonder if you could post me the book i lent you in november, i need it for some work i am trying to do while I cant move around much, do you remember which one im talking about, you borrowed it when you were writing that paper for your english class, if you could post it tomorrow or wednesday i will get it by friday

i hope everything is going well and that the person who was making life difficult for you at work has realised how silly shes being

love

angela

доставять
to deliver a baby –
рождать

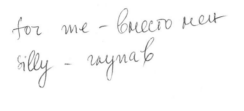

for me – вместо меня
silly – глупый

6 If you have Student's Cassette A, find Lesson 8, Exercise 1 (only the first part of the conversation is recorded here). Listen and write down at least ten words that have the letter *a* in them. Check with Student's Book Exercise 1.

"Hello, wall. Did you have a good day today? My big news is I discovered a new miracle washday product that has me all excited . . ."

---

9 People are different

1 Put in the correct verb forms.

1. I have got blue eyes, and so ....*has*.... my mother.
2. I haven't got a car, and neither ....*has*.. my husband.
3. English is a difficult language, and so ....*is*..... Russian.
4. Today's weather isn't very nice, and neither ....*was* yesterday's.
5. She can swim very well, and so ....*can*.... her sister.
6. I can't dance very well, and neither *can*........ my boyfriend.
7. Alice likes riding, and so ....*does*. Phil.
8. Marie doesn't speak English, and neither ..*does*.... Dominique.
9. Shakespeare lived in the 17th century, and so ....*did*.. Milton.
10. We didn't go to the meeting, and neither ..*did*.... most of the other people.

2 Put in *as* or *than*.

1. A diamond is harder *than*.... iron.
2. Wales is not as big ....*as*..... Scotland.
3. I work in the same office ..*as*........ my brother.
4. On average, women live longer *than*.... men.
5. Cheese has more calories ..*than*...... bread.
6. England is not nearly as big ...*as*...... New Zealand.
7. She plays much better *than*.... I do.
8. Your eyes are almost the same colour .....*as*..... mine.
9. I think football is far more interesting *than*.... tennis.
10. Eat ....*as*.... much .....*as*..... you like.

3 Look back at the pictures on pages 124 and 126 of your Student's Book, and complete these sentences with words from the box.

as	both	less	more	neither	so	than

1. Elizabeth is holding a book, and ...*so*... is Jeanne.
2. Elizabeth is slimmer ...*than*... Jeanne.
3. ...*Both*... of the women are sitting down.
4. Elizabeth is not holding a pen, and ...*neither*... is Jeanne.
5. Jeanne has got a hat on, and ...*so*... has Elizabeth.
6. Elizabeth looks ...*more*... happy ...*than*... Jeanne.
7. Jeanne has not got gloves on, and ...*neither*... has Elizabeth.
8. Elizabeth's clothes look ...*more*... expensive ...*than*... Jeanne's.
9. Elizabeth is not ...*as*... old ...*as*... Jeanne.
10. Jeanne isn't wearing a jacket, and ...*neither*... is Elizabeth.

4 Fill in the gaps with words from the box.

as	as	as much as	better	both	both of them
from	he	him	like	more	more	than	than
that	that	which

Helen could not decide ...*which*... of the boys she liked best. ...*2 Both of them*... were old friends of hers, and they ...*3 both*... had nice personalities. Rob was ...*more*... similar to her, perhaps. He had the same interests ...*5 as*... her, and they enjoyed doing things together. She was a bit older ...*6 than*... ...*7 him*..., but that was not very important. He was very grown-up and mature, and much more self-confident ...*8 than*... John. She was very fond of him, and she knew ...*9 that*... he loved her. Only she was not sure ...*10 that*... he loved her ...*11 as much*... John. John was very different ...*12 from*... her – he was not really ...*13 like*... anybody else she had ever met – and that made him ...*14 more*... interesting, in a way. He had travelled more than her, and ...*15 he*... could talk for hours about places that she had never seen. He was ...*16 better*...-looking than Rob, too – taller and stronger. And his eyes were the same colour ...*17 as*... the sea on a summer day. But John was strange. She never quite knew what he was thinking, and he sometimes did unexpected things that worried her.

5 Now continue the following text. Use the notes to help you.

Rob could not decide which of the two girls he liked best . . .

NOTES

Helen: similar to him; same interests; nice personality; old friend of his; older than him; sensible; pretty; in love with him.

Susan: very different from him; an unusual person; strange, fascinating personality; very intelligent; much younger than him; not so pretty as Helen; very beautiful eyes; probably not in love with him.

6 Write a few sentences about one of the following subjects.

1. Compare yourself and a person you know well.
2. What are the differences between people in the north and the south (or the east and the west) of your country?
3. Compare people from your country with the British or the Americans.

10 Things are different

1

Write your own ends for these sentences, using *as* or *than* correctly.

1. Maths is less interesting *than dreams*
2. Maths is more interesting *than swim*
3. English is not as easy *as bulgarian*
4. English is more useful *than russian*
5. A bicycle is less expensive *than a car*
6. A bicycle is not as fast *as a car*
7. A bicycle is more expensive *than tram*
8. I'm happier/older/taller *than you*
9. I'm not as happy/old/tall *as him*
10. This country is not as . . .
11. This country is less . . .
12. This country is . . .er/more . . .
13. My friend . . . is less . . .
14. The teacher is . . .

2

Write two sentences to compare each of the following.

a mouse and a cat

A mouse is smaller than a cat.

A cat can run faster than a mouse.

1. Britain and your country
2. the United States and the USSR
3. a car and a bicycle
4. men and women
5. yourself and another person

*dense populative –
густо населен

tennous – изгорнив
(tennis)*

"There goes a car with exactly the same number as ours."

3

Look at the two pictures. They are not quite the same. For example, in picture B the man's hair is longer. Can you find ten more differences? (The solution is on page 116.)

A   B

4

Choose the correct words to fill in the gaps in the sentences.

1. Your English is much *better* than mine. (*better/best*)
2. The *best* whisky comes from Scotland. (*better/best*)
3. We've had much .... rain this year than last year. (*more/most*)
4. The place that gets the .... rain in the world is a mountain in Hawaii. (*more/most*)
5. In the 'Cheap Round the World Race', the winner is the person who spends the *least* money getting round the world. (*less/least*)
6. I don't know much, but she knows even *less* than I do. (*less/least*)
7. Which month has the *fewest* days? (*fewer/fewest*)
8. There are .... Jews in Israel than in New York. (*fewer/fewest*)
9. 'Are you any good at tennis?' 'I'm the *worst* tennis-player in the world.' (*worse/worst*)
10. 'How's your headache?' 'It's getting *worse*.' (*worse/worst*)
11. 'I'll get you an aspirin. That'll make you feel *better*.' (*better/best*)
12. People say that Rolls-Royce cars are the *best* in the world. (*better/best*)

5

Strange but true! Read this with a dictionary.

The population of Mexico City is twice as big as the population of Norway.
Tortoises live longer than people; some bacteria live longer than tortoises. Some trees live for over 3,000 years.
In the 18th century a Russian woman had 69 children.
The world record for water-skiing is faster than the world record for downhill skiing.
The Olympic weightlifting champion Paul Anderson lifted 6,270 pounds (2,850 kilos) in 1957, in a 'backlift.' This is as heavy as three football teams plus five more men.
The nucleus of a hydrogen atom, multiplied 100,000 times, would be as big as this dot:•

6

If you have Student's Cassette A, find Lesson 10, Exercise 1 (only A and B are recorded here). Listen, and write down as much as you can.

turtle – водна костенурка   downhill – спускане

21

11 Stuff for cleaning windows

1 Put in suitable words or expressions.

1. I'd _like_ a shampoo for dry _hair_, please.
2. _Large_, medium or small?
3. 'How _much_ is that?' '65p.'
4. Can I _look_ round?
5. 'Can I help you?' 'I'm _being_ served, thank you.'
6. _Can_ I have _some_ aspirins, please?
7. _Anything_ else?' 'No, thank you. That's _all_.'

2 Match the things and their descriptions.

1. shoe polish
2. skis
3. gloves
4. glue
5. camera
6. razor

A. things for keeping hands warm – 3
B. stuff for sticking things – 4
C. a thing for taking pictures – 5
D. stuff for cleaning shoes – 1
E. a thing for shaving – 6
F. things for moving on snow – 2

3 Write descriptions (like the ones in Exercise 2) of these things.

a knife; soap; toothpaste; shaving-cream; a tin-opener.

Write descriptions of a few more things.

4 Find out the English names of ten things that you have bought recently. Learn them.

tin foods – консервирани храни

5 Read this with a dictionary and then answer the questions.

UP IN SMOKE

HOUSEWIFE Mrs Fay Funnell saved for months to buy a fur coat in the summer sales. Then after queuing for nine days she set fire to the coat, valued at £795 and bought by her in the sale for £79.

Astonished crowds, queuing outside Debenham's in Oxford Street, London, watched as 36-year-old Mrs Funnell burnt the coat.

As every woman's dream disappeared in smoke, she said: 'I am highly delighted. I hate the fur trade because it is cruel to animals. 150 minks have died to make this jacket.'

1. The text talks about Mrs Funnell in four different ways: *Housewife Mrs Fay Funnell*; *she*; *her*; *36-year-old Mrs Funnell*. The text also talks about her coat in four different ways. Can you find them and write them?
2. Do you think Mrs Funnell was right to burn the coat? (Write two or three sentences.)

6 If you have Student's Cassette A, find Lesson 11, Exercise 3. Listen to the sentences and practise the pronunciation.

"Yeah, they're all right, I'll take 'em."

22

12 I haven't got anything to wear

1 Fill in the blanks. Try to do the exercise *before* you look at the words in the box.

1. 'What's the _matter_?' 'I'm not feeling very well.' 'Oh dear. _Shall_ I get you an aspirin?'
2. 'Can you _lend_ me some money?' 'Yes, all right, I think _so_. When can you give it _back_ to me?'
3. 'Have you _got_ the time?' 'No, sorry, I'm _afraid_ I haven't.'
4. 'Would you like _to come_ to a party this evening?' 'That's very _kind_ of you. I'd love _to_.' 'All right. Can you _come_ to my house about 8 o'clock?'
5. 'Could I _borrow_ one of your dresses?' 'Yes, of course. Do you want _to borrow_ a pair of shoes to go with it?' 'Well, if you're sure you don't _mind_.'
6. 'Excuse me. _Could_ you tell me the _way_ to Times Square?' 'I'm sorry. I'm a _stranger_ here myself.'
7. 'Have you got _change_ for a £5 note?' 'Wait a _second_. I _'ll_ have a _look_.'

afraid	back	borrow	to borrow		change
come	to come	could	got	kind	lend
'll	look	matter	mind	second	shall
so	stranger	to	way		

2 Spelling: double letters. Put another letter in the blank if necessary.

pos_s_ible   nec_es_ary   let_t_er   visit_or
spel_l_ing   big_g_er   old_er   wait_ing
sit_t_ing   stop_p_ed   rub_b_ish   definit_ely

3 Infinitive with or without *to*?

1. I haven't got anything (_to eat_ / eat).
2. Why don't you (to take / _take_) a holiday?
3. I would like (_to go_ / go) out tonight.
4. 'That's the doorbell.' 'I'll (to go / _go_).'
5. Can you (to lend / _lend_) me some money?
6. That dress makes her (to look / _look_) funny.
7. I hope (_to see_ / see) you again soon.
8. Shall I (to carry / _carry_) that bag for you?
9. What time do you have (_to start_ / start) work in the mornings?
10. It's nice (_to see_ / see) you again.

4 Fill in the blanks in the text with words from the box.

after	again	ago	because	broken
called	deep	except	hit	hurt	lost
only	so	soon	started	stay	that
walking	when			

LOST – заблудиться

My sense of direction is not very good, and I easily get _lost_. One day, about ten years _ago_, I was _walking_ in the mountains between France and Italy _when_ the weather began to turn bad. I _started_ to make my way back downhill, _because_ I did not want to be caught in a storm. But after a few hundred metres I realised _that_ I was not sure of the way. The clouds came down lower and lower, it started to rain, and _soon_ I was completely lost.

I _called_ as loud as I could, but of course there was nobody close enough to hear me. I did not want to _stay_ on the mountain, but it was impossible to go on, _so_ I crawled into a hole between two rocks and waited for the storm to go over. _After_ two or three hours the rain stopped and the clouds lifted, and I was able to start walking _again_. I was very cold and hungry, and I had nothing to eat _except_ a few sweets.

About half an hour later I suddenly recognised my surroundings, and I realised that I was _only_ two or three hundred metres above the camp site. However, my troubles were not over. On my way down I slipped and _hit_ my knee against a rock. There was a _deep_ cut and it _hurt_ very badly, and as soon as I got back to the camp I went to see a doctor. Fortunately, nothing was _broken_.

5 Write about a time when you were lost, or write a story about somebody who was lost. Use words and expressions from Exercise 4, and from the text about Juliana Koepke on page 26 of the Student's Book.

6 If you have Student's Cassette A, find Lesson 12, Exercise 2 (only part of the conversation is recorded here). Listen to the conversation with the Student's Book closed and write down as much as you can.

Summary B

weare – стола (handwritten)

1 Put in the missing words.

1. She doesn't sing as well ...*as*... me. (handwritten annotation)
2. Your pronunciation is a lot better ...*than*... mine.
3. The meeting is at the same time ...*as*... last week.
4. My sister's personality is very different ...*from*... mine.
5. 'I didn't like the film much.' 'Neither ...*did*... I.'
6. 'Would you like to come to a party tomorrow?' 'I'd love ...*to*...'
7. A good motorbike costs nearly as much ...*as*... a car.
8. 'Did anything interesting happen?' 'I don't think ...*so*...'
9. I need some stuff ...*for*... cleaning silver.
10. 'I haven't got anything to wear.' 'What ...*about*... your blue dress?'
11. Why ...*don't*... you borrow something of mine?
12. '...*Shall*... I iron it for you?' 'Well, thanks very much. If you really don't ...*mind*...'

2 Choose the correct word.

1. Where's *my*/mine brother gone?
2. You can't take that bike. It's my/*mine*.
3. Ann and Johnny's garden is much nicer than our/*ours*.
4. 'Whose is that coat?' 'Your/*Yours*.'
5. They're nice people, but I don't like *their*/theirs friends.
6. Jane lost all *her*/hers baggage when she went to America.
7. If you show me *your*/yours holiday photos, I'll show you my/*mine*.

3 Put in *got* where it is correct.

1. Have you ...*got*... a light?
2. Goodbye. Have ...—... a good holiday.
3. I usually have ...—... lunch at one o'clock.
4. Excuse me. Have you ...*got*... the time?
5. I've ...*got*... three brothers.
6. Have you ...*got*... a few minutes? I'd like to have ...—... a talk with you.
7. 'What's the matter?' 'I've ...*got*... a headache.'
8. My parents have ...*got*... a small farm in Yorkshire.
9. Hello. Nice to see you. Sit down and have ...—... a drink.
10. She always has ...—... a bath before she goes to bed.

4 Write a short story using at least seven of the words from the box.

Christmas	helicopter	
beard	window	pram
shoe	police station	stuff
recognise	laugh	expensive
unusual	mine	less

5 Read this with a dictionary.

AFRICA'S PLEA — *мольба* (handwritten)

I am not you –
but you will not
give me a chance,
will not let me be *me*.

'If I were you –'
but you know
I am not you,
yet you will not
let me be *me*.   *Ефкан се* (handwritten)

You meddle, interfere
in my affairs
as if they were yours
and you were me.

You are unfair, unwise,
foolish to think
that I can be you,
talk, act
and think like you.

God made *me*.
He made *you*.
For God's sake   *за бога* (handwritten)
let me be *me*.

(Roland Tombekai Dempster)

"But you're special to me, darling."

6 Try the crossword.

(Solution on page 116.)

ACROSS

1. The opposite of *more*.
6. Very small person.
8. Hello (*informal*).
9. Have you got some .... for cleaning windows?
12. 'I don't agree with him.' '............... do I.'
14. The opposite of *under*.
15. What's .... phone number?
17. 'I like this music.' 'So .... I.'
18. *I am* in spoken English.
19. She speaks a lot .... languages.
21. 'What's the ....?' 'I've got a headache.'
23. It's white and it falls from the sky.
25. Not this.
26. 'What's your favourite colour?' '............... .'
28. One more time.
32. His eyes are the same colour .... mine.
33. Not any.
34. Children make a lot of ....
35. 'I'm tired.' 'So .... I.'
36. The past of *eat*.
37. Will not.
38. You can write with it.

DOWN

1. Could you .... me your raincoat?
2. It travels on the sea.
3. Please come in and .... down.
4. 'We haven't got any glasses.' 'It doesn't matter. We'll .... cups.'
5. 'Shall I help you?' '............... you really don't mind.'
7. It can fly.
10. .... the crossword.
11. I've been here .... about six weeks.
13. The place where you live.
16. 'Could I borrow your pen?' '............... course.'
18. What time is ....?
19. 'Where's my glass?' '............... the piano.'
20. The postman has just brought a letter .... you.
21. 'What does *post-structural* ....?' 'I have no idea.'
22. It travels on land, on rails.
23. You put this on a letter.
24. The past of *go*.
25. 'How was the party?' 'Not bad. Better .... usual.'
27. Ann likes opera, and so .... her boyfriend.
29. The present of *24 down*.
30. 'Jake isn't here yet.' 'Neither .... Sonia.'
31. Not old.
36. 'What's her job?' 'She's .... elephant trainer.'

"Come in, Ferguson. We were just talking about you."

Revision **B**

1 Vocabulary revision. How many words can you add in each group?

Buildings: house, station, *post, police*
Vehicles: car, *pram, train, bicycle*,
Clothing: jacket, *trousers, skirt, shirt, shoes*
Parts of the body: arm, *eyes, nose, ears,*
Furniture: table, *chair, armchair,*
Weather: rain, *snow, flash, wind, bread*
Food: meat, potato, *orange, egg, bread*
Jobs: driver, shop assistant, *dentist, nurse*

2 Grammar revision. Put in *a*, *some* or *one*.

1. 'Would you like ....*a*.... cup of tea?' 'Yes, thanks, I'd love ....*one*....'
2. Could I have ...*some*... shaving-cream, please?
3. 'What colour pen would you like?' '....*A*....
   red ...*one*..., please.'
4. I need ....*some*.... glue and ....*a*.... tin of black shoe polish, please.
5. We're looking for ....*a*.... fridge.
6. 'Have you got ...*some*.. packet of washing powder?' 'I've only got ....*a*.... small ...*one*...., I'm afraid.'

3 Stress. Write these words and underline the stressed syllables. Then practise saying them.
Example:

intelligence

above   afterwards   anyway   arrive   aspirin
century   Chinese   Christmas   difference
expensive   helicopter   material   (recognise) — *разнознавал*
remember   something   supermarket
together   unhappy   usual   village

skyscraper — небоскрёб
stool — табуретка
lightning = flash

4 Translate these into your language.

1. Can you lend me some stamps?
2. Excuse me. Have you got the time?
3. Can I borrow your pen?
4. Sorry, I'm afraid I'm using it.
5. Could you help me for a few minutes?
6. Well, I'm in a bit of a hurry.
7. Have you got a light?
8. Shall I post these letters for you?
9. Could I use your phone?
10. Would you like to play tennis this evening?
11. Could you tell me the way to the station?
12. I'll give you a hand with the cooking, shall I?

5 If you have Student's Cassette A, find Revision Lesson B, Listening Exercise 1 (only Marilyn's speech is recorded here). Make sure you know the words in the box; you can use your dictionary. Then listen to the recording and write down everything you hear.

comparison	resemble	angular	temperament

6 Write a comparison of two people you know well (for instance your mother and father, or two other people in your family, or two friends of yours).

"Have you seen a lady without me?"

13 Have you ever . . . ?

1 Put the correct verb form in each sentence.

1. When I was a child, I ~~never ate~~ cheese. (*never eat*)
2. ~~Have~~ you ever ~~lived~~ alone? (*live*)
3. Thousands of women ~~worked~~ in factories during the Second World War. (*work*)
4. ~~Did~~ you ever ~~have~~ a passport when you were a child? (*have*)
5. Jaime lives in Venezuela; he ~~has never seen~~ snow. (*never see*)
6. When your mother was at school, ~~did~~ she ~~have~~ to wear a uniform? (*have*)
7. I ~~came~~ to England in 1980. (*come*)
8. I ~~have lived~~ here ever since. (*live*)
9. What ~~did~~ your father ~~give~~ you for your last birthday? (*give*)
10. Shakespeare ~~never went~~ to university. (*never go*)
11. ~~Did~~ Napoleon ~~ever go~~ to China? (*ever go*)

2 Write ten interesting things that you have done in your life. Useful words: *seen, heard, been to, met, eaten, played.*

3 Write the contractions.

1. *It is* too hot. It's
2. The car *will not* start. won't
3. *She has* never been to Europe. she's
4. *She is* nearly eighteen. she's
5. I think *John is* hungry. John's
6. *I will* tell you tomorrow. I'll
7. *I would* like a holiday. I'd
8. Pat *has not* telephoned. hasn't
9. I *cannot* understand it. can't

Write the full forms.

1. It *doesn't* matter. does not
2. *Alan's* six feet tall. is
3. *She's* very thirsty. is
4. He says *he'll* pay. will
5. I *won't* go alone. won not
6. *She's* never met him. is
7. *We'd* like a table for two. would

4 Can you fill in the labels with words from the box? Use your dictionary to help you.

armchair	bookcase	carpet	ceiling	chair	curtain
door	fireplace	floor	lamp	light	piano	picture
plant	stereo	switch	table	wall	window	

16 table

27

5 If you have Student's Cassette A, find Lesson 13, Exercise 1 (only answers *b* and *e* are recorded here). Listen, and try to write down what you hear.

6 Read one or both of these texts, and do the exercise(s). You can use a dictionary.

A (Dick Francis writes thrillers – novels about crime and violence – that take place in the world of British horse racing.)

Dick Francis can't remember learning to ride: it came to him as naturally as learning to walk. Born in South Wales in 1920, he was a child star at horse shows and after six years' service in the RAF during the Second World War, he made his entry into racing as an amateur rider, becoming a professional National Hunt jockey in 1948. He rode for the Queen Mother and in 1953–4 was Champion Jockey.

Retiring in 1957, Dick Francis became racing correspondent for the Sunday Express and began writing. His first book, published that same year, was his autobiography, The Sport of Queens, which has recently been revised and updated. This was followed by a number of thrillers, the material for which he has gleaned principally from the racing world. Forfeit was awarded the Edgar Allan Poe Mystery Prize for the best crime story of 1969 in America. Whip Hand won the 1980 Crime Writers Association Gold Dagger award. Reflex was awarded the Edgar Allan Poe Mystery Prize for 1981.

He lives in America with his wife Mary, who helps with the research.

(Blurb from thrillers by Dick Francis)

When you have read the text, put the pictures in the correct order.

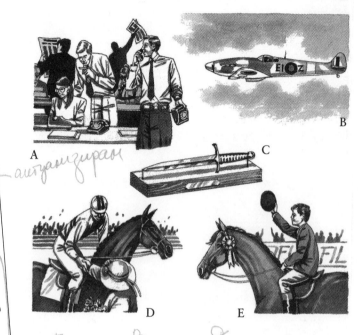

1. .... 2. .... 3. ....
4. .... 5. ....

B

Bernard and François Baschet are brothers. They live in Paris and work with new sounds and shapes for making music. They haven't always done this, though; for a long time Bernard managed a factory and François ran a business in Argentina. Then, about 30 years ago, they took their savings and began the work they do now. First they learnt all about how classical musical instruments were made, and then they began inventing their own instruments.

Now their lives are quite varied. They are still inventing new instruments; but Bernard has begun working with children as well. He helps them to discover music without having to read written notes. He sometimes travels, too, giving concerts on his instruments with other musicians. François also travels – sometimes to set up exhibitions, sometimes just for the pleasure of arriving in a new place.

Bernard's main complaint? The telephone. 'When an artist is working,' he says, 'and he has to run to the telephone, something is broken inside. I agree with the sculptor who said that freedom for the artist means having a secretary.'

Which is the most accurate summary of the text?

1. Bernard and François Baschet have spent a large part of their lives making new kinds of musical instruments.
2. The Baschet brothers both work at inventing new musical instruments and teaching children to play them.
3. Bernard and François Baschet have recently begun working with new musical instruments: they invent them, teach children to play them, give concerts and set up exhibitions.

14 Things have changed

grow older – остарбаш (handwritten)

1 Complete the table of irregular verbs.

INFINITIVE	PAST TENSE	PAST PARTICIPLE
go	went	gone / been
become	became	become
break	broke	broken
dream	dreamt	dreamt
drink		
eat	ate	eaten
fall		
feel		
find	found	found
get		
hit	hit	hit
learn		
lend	left	left
lie		
meet	met	met
ring	rang	
rise		
spend		
take	took	
tell	told	
wear		
win	won	won

2 Look at the pictures. What has happened to the man and woman since they were young?

shaters – шторы (handwritten)

3 Put *since* or *for* into the gaps.

1. since 1968
2. for twenty years
3. since Monday
4. for three days
5. for two months
6. since August
7. for three hours
8. since ten o'clock
9. for a long time
10. since yesterday
11. since my birthday
12. for two weeks
13. since last year
14. for a few minutes

4 Match the beginnings and ends (you can use a dictionary) and write out the complete descriptions. Example:

A ruin is a building that has fallen down.

A graduate is — somebody who has grown up.
An adult is — somebody who has beaten everybody else at a sport.
A champion is — somebody who has had an accident.
A casualty is — somebody who has finished university.
A ruin is — a child who has lost both parents.
Ice is — water that has covered the land.
A failure is — a building that has fallen down.
A flood is — water that has frozen. — *замрзшая* (handwritten)
An orphan is — somebody who has not succeeded in life.

тёрёть (handwritten)
leygarinek (handwritten)

5 Look around the room that you are in. Can you write down twenty words for things that you can see? Find out the names of five more things and learn them.

6 Write eight or more sentences about yourself. You can choose some of these ideas, or write about other things.

Do you feel strongly about any political question?
Have you ever done something that surprised your family or friends?
Have you changed very much in the last few years?
How important is cooking and eating food to you?
Is there a certain sort of music, or book, or other entertainment, that you like very much?
Were you happy or unhappy as a child?
Have your parents been an important influence in your life?
Have you ever been in love?

He left for good – замуж завитан (handwritten, circled)

use to be – Беше (било е) Нуман pape – пула (handwritten)

15 What do you say when you . . . ?

1 Put in one of the expressions from the box. (More than one answer may be possible in some sentences, but you must use all the expressions.)

a few	a little	any	enough	how many
how much	no	some	too	too much

1. Let's have a rest for .... minutes.
2. Can you turn down the TV? It's ~~too~~ loud.
3. There isn't ~~too~~ soup for four people. I'll have to make ~~some~~ more.
4. This tea isn't sweet ...., and there isn't .... milk.
5. I need a ~~little~~ time to think.
6. Could I have just a ~~little~~ more bread?
7. ~~How many~~ languages can you speak?
8. There hasn't been ~~any~~ snow this year.
9. .... money do you need?
10. Half the people in the world haven't got .... to eat, and half of the others eat ~~too much~~
11. There are ~~no~~ buses from our village on Sundays.

2 Here are typical expressions from four different situations. Can you sort them into four groups? (There is one expression that doesn't belong.) Can you think of any more typical expressions for the four situations? And what *are* the situations? Begin your answer like this:

Group 1: *Situation* <u>On the telephone</u>

Expressions <u>I'm afraid he's on the other line.</u>

I'm afraid he's on the other line.
Could I see the wine list?
Take-off is delayed for three hours.
Is that Andrew? This is Paul.
Can I try it on?
Would you like a little more sauce?
Have you got it in a larger size?
Would you ask her to call me back, please?
How much is it?
Which platform for Liverpool?
You can only take one piece of hand baggage.
Could you give him a message?
Is everything all right?
We have to go through a security check.
Could I have the bill, please?
Nothing to declare.
Can I look round?

3 Look at the pictures and write some things that the people could be saying. Example:

1. 'Could you check the tyres?'

1

2

3

4

5

6

7

8

4 Write the adverbs. Examples:

cold <u>coldly</u>

quiet <u>quietly</u>

easy   careful   happy   tired   complete
extreme   possible   soft   warm   beautiful
probable   nice

5 If you have Student's Cassette A, find Lesson 15, Exercise 4 (only the first five conversations are recorded here). Write down one or more of the conversations.

6 Read this with a dictionary.

RECORDS

When the spacecraft Apollo X was coming back to earth, it reached a speed of 24,791 miles per hour (39,897kph) – the fastest speed at which human beings had ever travelled.

In 1977, a New Zealander ran 5,110 miles (8,224km) in under 107 days.

In 1979, an American ran 50 metres in 18.4 seconds on his hands.

Also in 1979, a New Zealander ran 100 yards (91.7m) backwards in 13.1 seconds.

In 1978, a blind English runner ran 100 metres in 11.4 seconds.

In 1931–2, an American walked backwards from California to Turkey.

In 1984, 16 Japanese cyclists rode one bicycle at the same time.

The 24-hour record for walking backwards is 84 miles (135.18km).

The record for 1 mile (1.6km) on snowshoes is 7 minutes 56 seconds.

A man with one leg jumped 2.04 metres in 1981.

A man swam 1,826 miles (2,938km) down the Mississippi in 1930.

The record for non-stop balancing on one foot is 34 hours. The non-stop crawling record is 28.5 miles (45.87km).

A Russian fell 6,700 metres (21,980ft) from a plane without a parachute in 1942, and lived. A British flier jumped from a burning plane without a parachute in 1944, fell 5,500 metres (18,000ft), landed in a tree and a snowdrift, and was not hurt.

Some more records: dropping eggs without breaking them 650 feet (198m); throwing eggs without breaking them 96.9 metres; non-stop guitar playing 300 hours; non-stop talking 240 hours; making a suit 1 hour 34 minutes 33.42 seconds from sheep to finished suit (Australia 1982).

(Information from *The Guinness Book of Records*)

16 Here is the news

1 Look at the pictures. What has the person been doing in each one?

1 She has been writing letters

2

3

4

5

6

7

8

9

10

2 Answer these questions with *since* or *for*. Example:

How long have you been married?

For three months. / Since Christmas.

1. How long have you had the shoes that you are wearing now?
2. How long have you lived at your present address?
3. How long have you been at your present school?
4. How long have you known your English teacher?
5. How long have you been learning English?
6. How long have you had this book?
7. How long have you been doing this exercise?
8. How long have you known your doctor?
9. How long have you had your watch?
10. How long have you known your best friend?

3 Underline the stressed syllables. Examples:

<u>What</u> have you been <u>doing</u>?

<u>How</u> <u>long</u> have you been <u>working</u> <u>here</u>?

1. What have you been talking about?
2. How long have you been learning English?
3. Where have you been staying?
4. Why have you been crying?
5. The President has been visiting America.
6. John and I have been playing with the children.

4 Look out of the window. Can you write down twenty words for things that you can see? Find out the names of five more things and learn them.

5 If you have Student's Cassette A, find Lesson 16, Exercise 1 (only the second half of the news broadcast is recorded here). Read the following text and listen to the recording. Can you find fourteen differences?

The heavy rain which has been falling steadily for the past two weeks has caused widespread flooding. The River Fant has just burst its banks in West Milltown, and parts of the city centre are under water. The bad weather has ruined many vegetable crops, and food prices in San Fantastico have been going up steadily for the last week. The Minister for Consumer Affairs has just announced that price controls on vegetables and fruit will come into effect tomorrow.

Foreign exchange. The Fantasian grotnik has risen to its highest level against the Outland dollar since last July. The exchange rate is now 1.23 grotniks to the dollar.

The fire which has been burning in Grand South Station for the last five days is now under control. The origin of the fire, which started in the station toilets on Monday, is still unknown. Three more firemen were overcome by smoke during the night, and have been taken to hospital.

And now the weather. Light rain will continue in all parts of Fantasia, . . .

6 Write the text for a short news broadcast, using some of the following sentence-frames. (You can make some changes if you want to.)

The .... which has been ....ing for ....
has .... has just ...., and ....

.... has just .... has ....,
and ....

The .... has .... since ....
is now ....

Three .... (SIMPLE PAST) yesterday. The Minister .... has .... that ....

A .... has been ....ing in .... since
....

The Prime Minister / President has just ....
He/She has been ....ing ....

"Fifteen years we've commuted together on this train: fifteen years all we've ever said to each other has been 'Good Morning' – I'd just like you to know, I love you."

17 USA holiday

1 Complete these sentences using *may*.

1. If a small child plays with matches, *he or she may get burnt*

2. If you don't lock your car when you park it, . . .

3. If you don't put your name on your suitcase when you travel, . . .

4. If you drive after drinking too much alcohol, *you may get in a accident*

5. If you give a coin to a baby, . . .

6. If you smoke in bed, *you may get*

7. If a child walks around with a pencil in its mouth, *it may get hurt*

2 Put capital letters and punctuation marks where they belong.

one of my friends has just returned from a holiday in the usa. he now considers himself an expert on the states / it makes me laugh / but its not the first time ive seen it / people go to america with a firm idea of what theyre going to find there and then they find it. they dont meet many americans   because they never leave their own little group. they go to the tourist traps   disneyland and miami beach   for example   and follow their tour guides around like sheep. they are shown exactly what they want to see   and so they think that america really is exactly like its cinema image

i think the only way to get to know a country is to go there alone or in a very small group   and stay in a place where there are not very many tourists. then you have a chance of meeting people and finding out what their life is really like. of course   it is important to try and learn at least a little bit of the language before you go. you wont come back an expert   but you will know more than my friend knows about america

3 Travel verbs. Complete the table.

1. travel by air   = fly
2. travel by car   = drive
3. travel on foot   = walk
4. travel on horseback   = ride
5. travel by bicycle   = ride

4 In English, most two-syllable words are stressed on the first syllable, like this:

□□ rather   □□ difference   □□ Europe

Can you find five words in this list that are stressed on the second syllable?

awful   Britain   depend   dirty   enjoy   except
language   listen   living   noisy   people   ready
sincere   throughout   very

5 If you have Student's Cassette A, find Lesson 17, Exercise 4 (only the third speaker is recorded here). Try to write down everything you hear.

"She said will passengers for somewhere I didn't catch go to gate number something or other."

"Pardon me, we're from New Orleans – would you call this foggy?"

6 Read the directions and draw the route on the map.

WALK TO LONDON'S MUSEUMS

A Royal Albert Hall
B Imperial College
C Royal College of Music
D Science Museum
E Geological Museum
F Natural History Museum
G Victoria and Albert Museum

This walk starts at busy Marble Arch. Go west along the side of Hyde Park, parallel with Bayswater Road, as far as the pleasant water-gardens at the north end of the Serpentine. Walk south across the gardens, then continue down a tree-lined avenue (you are now in Kensington Gardens) to the elaborate Albert Memorial, built between 1864 and 1876 as a monument to Queen Victoria's beloved Prince Consort. The huge brick-coloured building across the road is the Royal Albert Hall, used broadmindedly (and at different times) for events as different as classical music concerts and wrestling matches. Cross Kensington Road to Queen's Gate, and then turn left into Prince Consort Road. Here you see the back of the Albert Hall and part of Imperial College and the Royal College of Music. Turn right into Exhibition Road. Two hundred yards along

you will reach the Science Museum, one of the great museums which owe their existence to the profits of the Great Exhibition of 1851. Beyond the Science Museum, which is especially recommended for children who are interested in seeing how things work, are the Natural History Museum and the Geological Museum. Across Exhibition Road is the most famous of the four, the Victoria and Albert Museum.

Walking time to the museums is about an hour.

At least two hours should be allowed for each of the museums you want to visit. Those not wanting to see the museums can walk along Brompton Road into the smart shopping area of Knightsbridge (Harrods is there). Museum-goers will do better to take a bus when they emerge into the daylight.

34

18 Knife-thrower's assistant wanted

1 Put in the missing words.

1. Ask him to phone me as soon _as_ possible, please.
2. She earns $50,000 _a_ year.
3. I look forward _to_ hearing _from_ you.
4. 'How often do you go to America?' '_Every_ three months.'
5. I used to _be_ very shy, but now I'm OK.
6. Would you like _a_ little more soup?
7. Fill up _with_ four-star, please.
8. I'd like a single room _for_ two nights.
9. The toilets are the first door _on_ the left.
10. That's very kind _of_ you.
11. 'Thanks very much.' 'Not _at_ all.'
12. She's not old enough _to_ drive.

2 Choose the correct tense (Present or Present Perfect).

1. We _know / have known_ each other for three years.
2. How long _do you live / have you lived_ here?
3. _I'm seeing Jake / I've seen Jake_ at six o'clock.
4. She _has / has had_ that job since 1985.
5. Sorry, the train was late. How long _are you waiting / have you been waiting_?
6. He _is starting / has started_ work on Tuesday.

3 times a day

3 Join beginnings and ends with _must_ to make six or more sentences.
Example:

A teacher must know how to make lessons interesting.

BEGINNINGS	ENDS
A teacher	like animals
A driver	be interested in money
A gardener	know how to make lessons interesting
A businessman	know how to change his or her voice
A photographer	be able to type
A secretary	be good at mathematics
An engineer	like selling
A vet	like children
A doctor	like working alone
A salesperson	like working with people
A writer	have a camera
An actor or actress	have a good sense of direction
A shop assistant	want to help people
A primary-school teacher	like working outside

"We're offering you the job on probation, Whitlock. You have three months to become one of us."

"I'm leaving you, Nora. The company has transferred me to another wife."

4 How many sentences can you write with words from the box? Each sentence must have two of the words in. You can make small changes to the words. Example:

I ate a lot of potatoes because I was hungry.

average	beautiful	believe	bird	boring	cheap	clothes
dangerous	down	dream	everybody	fourth	gun	
happy	hot	hungry	message	piano	picture	post
potato	problem	square	strange	sugar		

5 Underline the stressed syllables. Example:

experience

assistant   company   education   interview   advertise   unable   essential
excellent   necessary   between   several   possible   forward

6 Read the advertisements with a dictionary. Then write a letter of application for one of the jobs.

ADVERTISEMENTS

ROSTON TIMES

MANAGER
FOR SMALL NEWSAGENTS
Applicants must have experience of running a small shop. Good knowledge of accounting desirable. Aged 25–40. Apply in writing to: Personnel Manager Chambers and Wren Chambers House High Street Barbury BA6 10S.

FULL-TIME GARDENER
wanted for Roston General Hospital. Experience essential. Good wages and conditions. Apply: The Administrator.

RECEPTIONIST

Efficient
SHORTHAND TYPIST/ SECRETARY
needed for small friendly company. Apply to Office Manageress, Ann Harper Ltd, 6 Newport Road, Roston RS1 4JX.

CLEANER
required for our Roston office, hours by arrangement. Apply The Manager Coleman and Stokes 33 South Parade Roston RS1 5BQ.

PART-TIM
RECEPTION
for young, grow relations co specializing in local sm Apply to The Ro

Yours faithfully

Yours sincerely

Summary C

1 Look at the pictures. What has the person been doing in each one?

She has been riding... *He has been ating* *He has been aiming* *walking the dog* *he has been washing*

1

2

3

4

5

6

7

8

2 Put in *my, mine, your, yours, his, her, hers, our, ours, their* or *theirs.*

1. 'Excuse me, that's ....*my*.... coat.' 'Oh, is it? I'm sorry. I thought it was ..*mine*...'
2. We've got the same kind of house as Mr and Mrs Robson, but ..*theirs*.. is a bit bigger than ours.
3. Could we have ....*our*.... bill, please?
4. 'Is that Jane's cat?' 'No, this one's white. ..*Hers*.... is black.'
5. 'Have you seen ..*his*.... new motorbike?' 'Oh, it isn't ..*yours*.. He just borrowed it.'
6. 'When's ..*your*.. birthday?' 'December 15th.' 'Really? Mine's the day before ..*yours*..'
7. Mary and ..*her*.. boyfriend are taking ..*their*.. holiday in June – the same time as we're taking ..*ours*...... Why don't we all go together?

3 Which one is different? Why? Example:

car taxi pram bicycle
Bicycle – the others have four wheels.
OR *Taxi – you don't pay to use the others.*
OR *Pram – the only one that you push.*

1. coach car bicycle bus
2. train bicycle car motorbike
3. train car plane bus
4. walk ride hitchhike cycle
5. New York Las Vegas Tokyo Hawaii
6. river town city village
7. river swimming-pool sea lake
8. butcher's chemist's library bookshop

4 Write these words and underline the main stress. Then check in a dictionary and practise saying the words. Example:

advertise

agriculture apply assistant average avoid
become colony company continue
economy education election essential
excellent experience faithfully family
government hospital improve interview
necessary percentage population
qualification salary sincerely traffic
unemployment vegetable

5 Translate these into your language.

1. 'Have you ever been to Glasgow?' 'No, I never have.'
2. During the last three years, I have travelled about 100,000km.
3. How long have you known her?
4. The President and his wife <u>have</u> just <u>arrived</u> in Canada for a three-day visit.
5. What have you been doing this week?
6. I used to be very shy, but now I'm OK.
7. I'm afraid you've got the wrong number.
8. First on the right, second on the left.
9. Is service included?
10. 'That's very kind of you.' 'Not at all.'

6 Read this with a dictionary.

THE WORLD'S WORST DRIVER

The world record for the most traffic offences in the shortest period of time is held by a man from Frisco, in Texas, who achieved this feat in the first twenty minutes of car ownership.

Having hitch-hiked to the nearby city of McKinney on 15 October 1966, he bought a 1953 Ford and drove out of the used car showroom at 3.50pm.

At 3.54 he collided with a 1952 Chevrolet driven by a local woman, Mrs Wilma Smith Bailey, at the corner of McKinney and Heard Street.

One minute later he collided again 90 feet south of Virginia Street and Tennessee Street with another Chevrolet, driven by Miss Sally Whitsel of Farmersville.

Feeling more confident now in his new vehicle, he next drove round the courthouse one-way system in the wrong direction. Forty-six feet later he hit a 1963 Ford. It was still only 3.58.

He continued in this vein until 4.15pm, when he was in deep conversation with Patrolman Richard Buchanan, having just hit a Ford Mustang in Louisiana Street.

In the space of just 20 minutes he had acquired 10 traffic tickets, caused six accidents, hit four cars without stopping and driven on the wrong side of the road four times.

When questioned, this determined motorist, who had not driven for 10 years, said: "They don't drive like they used to".

(From *The Return of Heroic Failures* by Stephen Pile)

"Gloria, the travellers cheques!
Throw out the travellers cheques!"

Revision C

1 Match the countries and capitals. Use an atlas if necessary. Learn any of the English names that you don't know. Example:

Argentina – Buenos Aires

COUNTRIES
Argentina   Czechoslovakia   Denmark
Egypt   Germany   Greece   India
Indonesia   Iran   Ireland   Japan
The Netherlands   Nigeria
People's Republic of China   Poland   Portugal
Switzerland   Taiwan   Thailand   Turkey
The USSR   Yugoslavia   Zaire

CAPITALS
Amsterdam   Athens   Bangkok   Beijing
Belgrade   Berne   Buenos Aires
Cairo   Copenhagen   Delhi   Djakarta
Dublin   Berlin   Ankara   Kinshasa   Lagos
Lisbon   Moscow   Prague   Taipei   Tehran
Tokyo   Warsaw

2 Put in *can, cannot, may, may not, will, will not* or *must.*

1. Most birds .... fly.
2. Most animals .... fly.
3. We .... be a bit late this evening – I'm not sure.
4. If you go to Scotland for a holiday, you probably .... spend all your time sunbathing.
5. Secretary wanted – .... speak good English.
6. If you speak your own language in England, most people .... understand you.
7. If you speak English in Canada, most people .... understand you.
8. We don't know if we can go on holiday this year. We .... have enough money.
9. I don't know if I .... help you.
10. A professional pianist .... practise for several hours every day.

38

3 Complete the table of irregular verbs.

INFINITIVE	PAST TENSE	PAST PARTICIPLE
bring	*buy*	
brought	bought	
brought	*bough*	chosen
come		
come	flew	
come	*flew*	forgotten
hold		
held	left	
held		lost
mean		
meant	ran	
meant		sold
sing		
sang	swam	
sung		woken

4
If you have Student's Cassette A, find Revision Lesson C, Grammar Exercise 1. Listen to the song again and try to write the first two verses. Check in your Student's Book to see how much you have understood correctly.

5
Write the text for a short news broadcast. All the news must be good. Some things that you could put in: a demonstration; a visit by an important person; a birth; a marriage; a sports report; a weather report.

6 Try the crossword.

DOWN
1. The people who work in a place.
2. 'Where's Rosie?' '............... bed.'
3. Fred doesn't smoke .... drink.
4. Not old.
5. We have these every five years, to choose Members of Parliament.
6. The opposite of *hard*.
7. Not hot; not warm.
8. 'Fill up with unleaded, please.' 'Right. And shall I check the ....?'
9. '............... I iron your dress for you?' 'If you really don't mind.'
13. I'll come back as soon as ....
15. Animal that drinks milk, catches mice and doesn't like dogs.
16. .... you go on holiday to Texas, you won't do much skiing.
17. Half past .... is halfway between a quarter past five and a quarter to eight.
19. Your mother's son's mother's husband's daughter's father's brother is your ....
20. The sky may be this colour.
22. To get a really good job, you probably .... both qualifications and experience.
24. Sorry I'm .... Have you been waiting long?
25. Very hard cold water.
26. Animal that doesn't like *15 down*.
29. What time .... the first buses run in the morning?
30. The opposite of *happy* is *......happy*.
31. Not any.

(Solution on page 116.)

ACROSS
1. The opposite of *long*.
3. Fifty-two weeks = ... year.
6. Yours ....
9. My parents were both born in March, and ......*so*... was I.
10. You and I.
11. Yours ....
12. You can drink out of it.
14. She lives .... 37 Cumberland Street.
15. You can do this with a knife.
16. I don't know where my coat ....
18. If you want a good job you may need these.
21. If you want to drive, you must have a driving ....
23. Not young; not new.
27. This is useful for seeing.
28. You can get this at school.
32. Past participle of *do*.
33. Excuse me, have you .... a pen that I can borrow?

19 Their children will have blue eyes

1 Match the beginnings and ends of the sentences.

If you are travelling at 80kph in a car,
If the score in your game is 40–15,
If today is your golden wedding anniversary,
If your great-grandparents all had blue eyes,
If you travel from England to Scotland,
If last year was a leap year (with 366 days),
If you can speak French,
If you can see pink elephants,

next year won't be a leap year.
you have been married for 50 years.
you can understand at least a bit of Italian.
perhaps you need to see a doctor.
you have blue eyes.
you can stop safely in 52m.
you do not go through customs and immigration.
you are probably playing tennis.

2 Where will you be this time tomorrow? This time next week?
A month from now? This time next year? Write sentences.

This time tomorrow I will be . *at the English course , (in class)*
This time next . . .
A month . . .
This . . .

3 Write sentences with *will certainly, will probably,
may, will probably not* or *will certainly not.*
Example:

Will you be in the same house this time next year?

I will probably not be in the same house
this time next year.

1. Will you live to be 100 years old?
2. Will next year be better for you than this year?
3. Will it rain this evening?
4. Will you do all the exercises in this book?
5. Will you sleep well tonight?
6. Will you get a lot of presents on your birthday?
7. Will you climb a mountain during the next
   twelve months?
8. Will doctors discover a cure for cancer before
   the year 2000?
9. Will there be a world war in the next ten years?
   (Start *There will/may . . .*)
10. Will you be able to speak perfect English
    one day?
11. Will you be able to dance when you are 90?
12. Will you have to get up early tomorrow?
13. Will you have to work next weekend?

4 Do you know the names of all these containers?
Write them down, using a dictionary if necessary.
Learn the ones you didn't know.

40

5 Here are some sentences about things that may happen in the future. Read the sentences with a dictionary, and decide which developments will do most good to the world. Write down the letters of the sentences in order of importance.

A. If people take a special drug, they will be able to eat as much as they like without getting fat.

B. There will be a vaccine which will stop teeth going bad – people will never have toothache.

C. There will be drugs which will stop us feeling pain, but will not make us unconscious.

D. People will be able to live 20–40 years longer than now.

E. Women will be able to have children at the age of 60.

F. We may be able to partly control the weather.

G. Trains will be able to travel at 2,000 kph in special vacuum tunnels.

H. Translating machines will be so good that nobody will have to learn foreign languages.

Order of importance: 1. ___E___ 2. ___C___ 3. ___B___
4. ___H___ 5. ___A___ 6. ___D___ 7. ___F___ 8. ___G___

6 Read these with a dictionary.

'When I was a kid, I had no watch. I used to tell the time by my violin. I used to practise in the middle of the night and the neighbours would yell "Fine time to practise the violin, three o'clock in the morning!"'

(Henny Youngman)

'Insanity is hereditary, you can get it from your children.'

(Sam Levenson)

'Anybody who hates children and dogs can't be all bad.'

(W. C. Fields)

'I think my husband has been unfaithful to me. My last child didn't look like him at all.'

(Ann Smith)

'We're paid to get on with the children. They aren't paid to get on with us.'

(Teacher at the Dragon School, Oxford)

'Father heard his children scream,
So he threw them in the stream,
Saying as he drowned the third,
"Children should be seen, *not* heard!"'

(Harry Graham)

A woman wrote to the famous dramatist George Bernard Shaw, saying 'You have the greatest brain in the world and I have the most beautiful body; so we ought to produce the most perfect child'. Shaw replied 'Yes, but if it was born with my beauty and your brains?'

"You'll wait for me and try to be faithful? Dammit – I'm only in for 30 days."

"You'll like Mum and Dad – they're out!"

41

20 A matter of life and death

1 Look at the pictures and say what is going to happen.

1

2

3

4

5

6 *to rob a bank*

7 *bring window*

8 *I's going to rain*

2 Report the sentences, beginning *She said . . .*
Examples:

'I'll be at home tomorrow.'

She said (that) she would be at home
tomorrow.

'You'll be late.'

She said (that) I would be late.

'Mary's going to have a baby.'

She said (that) Mary was going to have
a baby.

1. It will probably rain.
2. I'm going to see Anna.
3. It's late.
4. Jack's going to change his job.
5. I won't be at school on Friday.
6. There will be a meeting next Tuesday.
7. Alice and Rita are going to buy a car.
8. I'll always love you.
9. You'll forget me. *would forget me*
10. Prices are going to go up next week.
    were going

3 Spelling revision. Write the contractions.

1. I am I'm
   you are
   he is
   she is
   it is
   we are
   they are
2. I am not
   you are not
   she is not

3. there is
   there is not
4. do not
   does not
5. did not
6. have not
   has not

7. I will
   you will
   he will
   it will
   we will
   John will
8. cannot
9. I would
10. should not

4 If you have Student's Cassette B, find Lesson 20, Exercise 5 (only the first speaker is recorded here). List the numbers 1 to 20 on a piece of paper; listen to the recording and write the words that are missing from the text.

Well, we've decided that we're going to ......1...... ten kilograms ......2...... And we're going to ......3...... two blankets, one kilogram of dried ......4......, two backpacks and the ......5...... Erm, we're going to ......6...... sic –, we're going to take six ......7...... of ......8...... ......9...... Erm, we're going to take the ......10...... We're going to take the ......11...... We're going to take ......12...... in case of erm, ...13...... We're going to take the ......14...... ......15...... ......16...... We're going to take two ......17...... of ......18...... We're going to take a ......19...... and we're going to take two signal flares ......20......

5 We asked two soldiers who are trained in survival to do Exercise 3 in the Student's Book. Read their solution and the reasons for it. You can use a dictionary.

I think it is going to take us about five days to get to the nearest village. If both of us are fit, the woman can carry 15kg and the man can carry 20kg – don't forget that the packs are going to be lighter every day as we eat and drink. We are going to travel at night in the desert (using blankets for warmth) and sleep in turns during the day (under a blanket 'tent'). In the mountains we are going to travel during the day and sleep at night. Before we begin walking on the first day we are going to eat, and have a good drink of water.

Some things we are **not** going to take are:
– tent: too heavy, and we can use the blankets for a tent
– cooking equipment: we can cook and eat food from the tins
– radio receiver: we can't transmit
– rifle: we don't want to frighten people who see us
– tin opener: there's one on the knife

Here's what we're going to take:
– 2 backpacks
– rope (to make tent, to climb in mountains)
– 4 blankets (to make tent in the desert, for warmth when it's cold)
– 5 signal flares
– 12.5 litres of water
– torch and batteries
– 9kg of tinned food (to eat, possibly without cooking, from the tin)
– first aid kit (taking contents out of box)
– 0.2kg of newspapers (for 'floor' of tent)
– map
– compass
– sun cream
– 1kg of dried fruit (to eat in small portions for quick energy)
– knife
– sunglasses
– matches

6 Look again at Student's Book Exercise 3. Now write a similar problem yourself. It can be about somebody who is in trouble in the Arctic, or on the moon, or on a small island, or somewhere else – you decide.

21 If you see a black cat, . . .

1 Grammar revision. Complete the table of irregular verbs.

INFINITIVE	PAST TENSE	PAST PARTICIPLE
break	....	....
braue	burnt	....
Brouen	....	drawn
fall	....	....
....	got	....
hurt	....	hit
hurt	....	....
huet	meant	....
see	....	....
saw	shut	....
seen	....	stolen
throw	....	....
threw	won	....

2 *If* or *when*?
1. _When_ I get enough money, I'll buy myself a new car.
2. The house is so big – it's a bit frightening at night _when_ it's dark.
3. I suppose I'll have more time to myself _when_ the children get older.
4. _If_ it rains this afternoon, we won't have to water the flowers this evening.
5. _When_ a stranger offers you a ride home from school in his car, just say 'No, thank you' and walk straight on.
6. My mother is going to move to the country _if_ she retires.
7. _If_ I live to be 100, I'd like to have an enormous party.
8. You'll feel much better tomorrow _if_ you go to bed early tonight.
9. _When_ you go to bed tonight, could you leave the kitchen light on?
10. I don't think life will be worth living _if_ there is a third world war.
11. We'll have an easier time with money after November, _when_ we finish paying for the car.
12. Monica usually brings her cat _when_ she comes to visit us.

3 Put in the correct verb tenses.

1. I ___will come___ and see you tomorrow if I ___have___ time. (*come; have*)
2. I ___will phone___ you when I ___arrive___. (*phone; arrive*)
3. If it ___'s___ a warm night, we ___'ll have___ the party in the garden. (*be; have*)
4. Do you think you ___'ll find___ a job when you ___leave___ school? (*find; leave*)
5. If you ___'re___ hungry, tell me and I ___'ll get___ you something to eat. (*be; get*)
6. If you ___give___ me the keys, I ___'ll bring___ your car round to the front door. (*give; bring*)
7. When I ___have___ time, I ___'ll buy___ myself some new clothes. (*have; buy*)
8. If it ___rain___ at the weekend, we ___'ll stay___ at home. (*rain; stay*)
9. If Mother ___comes___ on Sunday, I ___'ll make___ a lemon meringue pie. (*come; make*)
10. When I ___stop___ work, I ___'ll travel___ round the world. (*stop; travel*)

4 Vocabulary. How many of these do you know the names of? Use a dictionary if necessary; learn the words you didn't know.

cow   sheep   dog   cangaroo
horse
pick   lion
elephant   whale
fly   spader   frog   snake   phish
ladybird – коровка
firefly – светлячок

5 If you have Student's Cassette B, find Lesson 21, Exercise 5. Listen to the recording and decide whether the following sentences are true or false.

1. John orders four bottles of champagne.
2. Olga wants to go to the zoo.
3. Olga has a green bag.
4. John finds Olga's address in her bag.
5. John doesn't go to the police.
6. John gets back to the office at five o'clock.
7. John takes £10,000 from the office safe.
8. At the airport, John sees Olga again.

"All creatures great and small: this is the Lord speaking! I want you all to get to bed early tonight. You're going to have a **big** day tomorrow!"

6 Reading skills. Read the text; don't use a dictionary. Then find the words *great*, *count*, *about*, *odd*, *custom*, *anxious* in the text. Each of these words can have several different meanings. Read the explanations and choose the meanings that the words have in the text.

great   1. very important
             2. very big
             3. well known
             4. good and enjoyable

count   1. If you count you are important.
             2. find out how many there are
             3. a kind of lord

about   1. If you're about to do something, you're going to do it soon.
             2. not exactly
             3. on the subject of
             4. round in a circle

odd   1. Odd numbers are 1, 3, 5, 7 etc.
             2. strange
             3. not happening very often

custom   1. thing that people like to do at certain times or in certain situations
             2. If you go to a foreign country, you may have to open your luggage at the customs.
             3. the people who use a shop

anxious   1. afraid, nervous about something
             2. not calm or relaxed
             3. If you are anxious to do something, you want to do it.

LOVE IS AN INSIDE-OUT NIGHTIE
Girls! Here's a great way to find out the name of your future husband.

According to an old superstition, you will dream of your husband-to-be if you –
Wear your nightie inside out.
OR *sleep with a mirror under your pillow.*
OR *count nine stars each night, for nine nights.*
OR *rub your bedposts with a lemon.*
OR *eat 100 chicken gizzards.*
OR *fill your mouth with water and run three times round the houses.*

The first man you see as you run will have the same name as your future spouse.

If you don't believe me, ask researcher Alvin Schwartz.

He's about to publish a book called Cross Your Fingers, Spit In Your Hat – a collection of the superstitions and odd customs people use to help them through life.

And he has found that we're just as anxious to court Lady Luck as any other generation.

We don't just believe old wives' tales – we're busy making up new ones.

Mr Schwartz says: 'We rely on superstitions for the same reasons people always have.

When we are faced with situations we cannot control – which depend on luck or chance – superstitions make us feel more secure.'

(John Hill, *Sun*)

nightie: night-dress
gizzard: part of a bird's digestive system
spouse: marriage partner
superstition: belief in luck, magic, etc.
court: try to get the favour of
old wives' tales: superstitions

---

22 We don't get on well

1 Put the words in the right order.

1. for to work easy she's
2. very talk he's to to difficult
3. work he's with nice to
4. with live to easy she's
5. music pleasant listen this is to to
6. with get to on easy she's
7. pleasure it's work a her with to

2 Use one or more words from the lesson in each blank.

1. My ex-girlfriend and I used to have a lot of rows; but when my new girlfriend and I have a ...., we talk about it.
2. I am very patient with young children, but I often .... angry with adults.
3. My brother Phil is very easy .... to.
4. I was sorry .... that your mother was ill.
5. Before I came to England, I didn't .... how different it was from other European countries.
6. Keith's .... his mind: he's not going to America for his holiday, he's going to Greece instead.
7. I was .... that house prices were going down.
8. Marilyn .... angry for silly reasons sometimes.
9. She's a lovely person; it's .... to work with her.
10. I like American food, but I can't .... American beer.

pencil sharpener – octpuncas

3 What did they say?

SUE: I like working with Paula.

She said (that) she liked working with Paula.

DAVE: She isn't always easy to get on with.

He said (that) she wasn't always easy to get on with.

SUE: She's very fair.
DAVE: She doesn't like to hear about her mistakes.
SUE: She tells interesting stories.
DAVE: She doesn't always tell true stories.
SUE: She listens very well.
DAVE: She tells everyone else everything she hears.
SUE: Dave, you're not being fair.
DAVE: I don't like people who are cleverer than me.

4 If you have Student's Cassette B, find Lesson 22, Exercise 6. Listen and repeat, trying for good intonation.

5 Write about somebody you know well; use a lot of words and expressions from the lesson.
OR: Imagine you live with a famous person. Write about how you get on with the person.

6 Put the past tense form of one of these verbs in each blank. Sometimes more than one answer may be correct.

hear	come	put	know	lose	tell
say	see	begin	make	go	can
have					
wake up					

1. When I .... yesterday it was raining.
2. I .... Janet at the disco last night.
3. John .... Prince when he was a boy.
4. I .... the same voice teacher as Pavarotti.
5. He .... his jacket on the bed, I think.
6. He .... he .... a headache, but I think he just didn't want to come.
7. How many people .... to the meeting last night?
8. When she was younger she .... run much faster than that.
9. They .... to Bali for two weeks in September.
10. Who .... you they were here?
11. I .... some people in the street at midnight last night.
12. I .... studying English when I was twelve.
13. I .... a terrible mistake yesterday.
14. Karen .... her glasses when she was in Spain.

"This could be difficult. They say they're all together."

---

23 If I were you, . . .

1 Complete the dialogue with the past or conditional (with _would_) of the verbs in the box. You should use some verbs more than once.

A: I can't think what to do. If John ....1.... here, he ....2.... what to do.
B: If I ....3.... you, I ....4.... the instruction book.
A: I've read it twice already, but I can't understand anything. Do you think it ....5.... a good idea if I ....6.... the top off and ....7.... inside?
B: I don't know. I don't think I ....8.... that if it ....9.... mine.
A: Well, what ....10.... you ....11.... if you ....12.... a problem like this?
B: I ....13.... John.
A: Well, that ....14.... easier if I ....15.... his number.
B: 61432.

be	do	have	know	look	phone	read	take

2 _Should_ or _would_?

1. If I were you, I ....n't do it like that.
2. I think you .... phone the police.
3. .... you like a cup of tea?
4. It .... be better if you turned it upside down.
5. I think everybody .... stop smoking.
6. Ann said that she .... be here at six o'clock, but she isn't.
7. People ....n't drink and drive.
8. What .... you do if you won a million dollars?

3 How many things are wrong in the picture? Example:

The cakes are upside down.

(handwritten margin notes: coat hanger зашараша; arrow-стрелка; oilwell — нефтяной варяженец; lottery — лото)

4 If you have Student's Cassette B, find Lesson 23, Exercise 2. Listen and practise the pronunciation of some of the sentences. Then listen again with the Student's Book open at page 70, and try to find all the differences.

5 Try to fill in the gaps in the letter without looking at the words in the box. Then look at the box for help with the words you could not guess.

```
Dear Al,
 ...1... a lot for your last letter. ...2... I ...3... answered
before; I've ...4... very busy getting ready to go to New York.
  I was really sorry ...5... about your trouble with Sally,
especially because it's ...6... going on for so long. You ...7...
try to make a decision soon, I think - it's bad for ...8... of
you to go on like this. I think perhaps it would ...9... if you
separated, but of course I might be ...10... - I don't know Sally
very well.
  You know, if ...11... I'd go away for a couple of ...12... . If
you were ...13... you could think things out ...14... and decide
what to do. ...15... take your holiday now and go off to Scotland
or somewhere like that? I'm ...16... it would do you a lot of good.
  Write again ...17... and let me know how things are going. And
don't ...18... to kiss Julie for me.
  Ann sends her ...19...
  Yours,
```

be better	been	been	both	calmly	by yourself	forget
haven't	to hear	I were you	love	should	soon	Sorry
sure	Thanks	weeks	wrong	Why don't you		

6 A friend of yours has a problem. For example: he or she doesn't like his or her job; or is having trouble with a parent/child/wife/husband/lover; or has money problems; or can't decide what to do after leaving school. Write a short letter giving your opinion. Use some of the words and expressions from Exercise 5 and from the Student's Book lesson.

47

24 How about Thursday?

1 Complete the conversation.

SARAH: Hello, Steve. *This* ...1... is Sarah. How are you?
STEVE: OK. ...*What* 2... about you?
SARAH: Oh, I'm ...3... . Listen, Steve. I'm having a party this weekend. Are you ...4... on Sunday?
STEVE: Saturday? Well, it's a ...5... difficult. I'm ...6... Ann and her family in the evening.
SARAH: No, Sunday.
STEVE: Oh, I'm sorry. I *'m be* 7 Saturday. Sunday might be OK. It ...8... ...9... time?
SARAH: Oh, any time after eight.
STEVE: I can't manage eight, but I'll come a bit ...10... . Say, nine.
SARAH: That's fine. Any time you like.
STEVE: Where?
SARAH: My ...11... . Bring a bottle.
STEVE: OK. Thanks *at 12el*. *see you 13* then.
SARAH: Bye.

2 Put in the right prepositions: *in, on, at, before* or *until*.

1. 'When's your birthday?' '...*In*... two weeks.'
2. I'll see you again ...*on*... Tuesday.
3. I'll be on holiday from tomorrow ...*until*... the end of August.
4. Goodnight. See you ...*in*... the morning.
5. I must finish this letter ...*before*... four o'clock, or I'll miss the post.
6. Hurry up – the train goes ...*in*... ten minutes!
7. The next meeting will be ...*on*... June 20th.
8. I'll be late for work ...*on*... Monday – I've got to go to the dentist.
9. 'Can I speak to Janet?' 'I'm afraid she's away ...*until*... next week.'
10. Could you look after the children *before* / *until* supper time?
11. I'm seeing the dentist ...*at*... ten o'clock.

3 Imagine that you are doing some of these things tomorrow. Say how long they will take you. Example:

It will take me half an hour to wash my hair.

> wash your hair   write to your mother   clean the kitchen   make a cake
> do your ironing   wash your car   pack your suitcase   go to the station
> run 1,500 metres   drive twenty km   play three sets of tennis
> learn twenty irregular verbs

4 Vocabulary. How many of these do you know the names of? Use a dictionary if necessary. Learn the words you didn't know.

5
If you have Student's Cassette B, find Lesson 24, Exercise 2 (only the first conversation is recorded here). Listen to the conversation and practise the pronunciation.

6
What are you doing next weekend or next week? Write 100 words or so.

"How about Thursday night, then?"

48

Summary D

1 Underline the stressed syllables. Example:

<u>some</u>body

about   accident   animal   appointment   beginning   certainly
complicated   depend   difficult   future   gardening   grandchild
hospital   million   parent   practise   probably   religion
until   vegetarian

2 Look at the pictures and say what will happen. Begin 'When . . .' Example:

'When she opens the door, the light will go on.'

3 Do you know how to form the past tenses (and past participles) of regular verbs? Try these verbs. If you have trouble remembering the rules, they are on page 116.

join joined

apply   cry   explain   fit
fix   guess   happen   hate
mend   need   play   start
stay   stop   wait

4 Put one of the words from the box into each blank.

at	from	in	into	of	off	on	over	through
to	under	with						

1. Do you eat melon .... a spoon or a knife and fork?
2. Ask the bus driver to tell you where to get ....
3. Shall we meet ....at.... the cinema?
4. Concorde flies ...over..... our house twice a day; it makes a terrible noise.
5. Rob jumped ......into.... the swimming pool with all his clothes on – he must have been drunk!
6. Some of the marchers threw stones at the police; one stone went through.... the window of a police car, and hit a policewoman on the head.
7. 'Do you know where my keys are?'   'I think they're ...on.... the table ...in... the kitchen.'
8. A lot ...of.... the people in our village work with horses.
9. We're going ...to.... France for our summer holidays.
10. People ...from.... warm countries generally have a hard time getting used to the winter in England.
11. I didn't see the cat when I walked into the room, because it was under the bed.

49

5 Translate some or all of these sentences into your language.

1. Why do people look like their parents?
2. Carol and Lee's baby may be tall.
3. I hope my children will be good-looking.
4. Maria said that I would never get married.
5. We're going to crash!
6. I think we should take a lot of water with us.
7. We're not going to take any blankets.
8. If you see a black cat, you'll have good luck.
9. When I go to London, I'll visit Sue.
10. If I go to Scotland, I'll visit Ann.
11. If I get enough money, I'll travel round the world.
12. What do you think of the new boss?
13. I get on all right with my boss.
14. I didn't realise that you didn't like your job.
15. If I were you, I'd turn it upside down.
16. I'd like you to meet my mother.
17. See you on Thursday. Bye.
18. I'd like to make an appointment to see Dr Gray.
19. Tuesday's a bit difficult. What about Thursday?
20. Let me look in my diary.

6 Write about your plans for this evening / tomorrow / the weekend. Example:

This evening I'm going to stay in and wash my hair. We're going to spend the weekend in the mountains.

"You ought to take a rest and forget all about windows for a while, Ted."

Revision D

1 Put in the correct verb forms.

1. We .... anything until we hear from you. (*not do*)
2. I'll tell you when I .... (*know*)
3. If I .... George, I'll tell him to come and talk to you. (*see*)
4. I .... happy when this job is finished. (*be*)
5. What .... if the police find out? (*happen*)
6. It'll be nice when we .... back home again. (*get*)
7. I .... your luggage until you come back. (*look after*)
8. When you decide to leave, phone us and we .... a flight for you. (*reserve*)
9. I'm going to take a short holiday when I .... this job. (*finish*)
10. Don't forget to put the lights out when you .... to bed. (*go*)

2 Put *when* or *until* in each blank.

1. Could you let me know .... Ms Amis arrives?
2. I can't give you an answer .... I hear from my bank.
3. .... the post comes, could you see if there's a letter from Emma in it?
4. Could you wait .... the children get home from school?
5. Eric's mother will be staying with us .... Christmas.
6. Who's going to look after your dog .... you go to America?
7. .... you make mayonnaise, you should make sure the oil and the egg are both at the same temperature.
8. Just keep straight on .... you see a big church; then take the first turning on the right.
9. I'll wait for you .... 9.00; if you haven't come by then, I'll know you have missed the train.
10. Don't try to get off the train .... it is moving.

3 Circle the word in each group that is different, and write why.

1. kettle   saucepan   (plate)   frying-pan
   You can cook in the others.
   OR: *You don't eat out of the others.*
2. wheel   plate   (shoe)   penny
3. cow   pig   (fish)   chicken
4. middle   (both)   side   end
5. grandchild   uncle   (friend)   mother
6. (heavy)   red   green   purple
7. pants   shirt   trousers   (wear)
8. boss   (office)   postman   driver
9. (film)   newspaper   letter   book
10. bus   train   lorry   (armchair)

4 If you have Student's Cassette B, find Revision Lesson D, Listening Exercise 3. Listen to the song and try to write down the first verse (**up to** *I just don't know . . .*). Check on Student's Book page 124.

5 *Strange but true!* Read this with a dictionary.

About 5,700 stars can be seen on a clear night without a telescope.
If you live in an old house in the country, you may be sharing your house with up to 3,000 animals and insects.
A mole takes about eight hours to tunnel 100 metres.
Diamonds and coal are made of the same chemical element.
Baby whales increase their weight by ten pounds an hour.
During a lifetime, a person's heart pumps enough blood to fill the fuel tanks of 2,100 Boeing 747s.
You get taller when you are asleep.
There were ten days in the ancient Egyptian week.
The silk made by spiders is stronger than steel.

"Look, I should sit down. Have you got a drink? Now it's nothing to worry about, really it isn't . . ."

"I love you for what you are – rich."

" . . . And here is the weather picture for noon tomorrow."

6 Try the crossword.

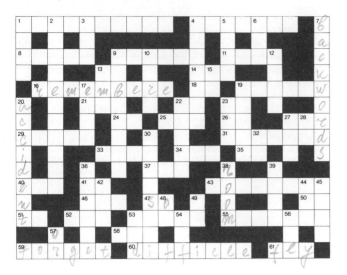

(*Solution on page 116.*)

ACROSS

1. Child's child.
4. When I make a ...., the boss gets angry.
8. I'm going to .... for a new job.
9. Your sweater's .... out.
11. 'What are you doing?' 'Trying to .... my bike.'
13. See you .... Thursday.
14. Thing at the end of your foot.
16. Tuesday's a bit .... – how about Thursday?
18. See you .... a couple of hours.
19. You can look out of this.
21. Not .... birds can fly.
22. Would you like .... orange?
23. Tea .... coffee?
24. I usually get .... at six o'clock.
25. A baby bird comes out of this.
26. There are .... people living on the moon.
27. You can drive this.
29. An animal that lives in the desert.
31. Scotland is not part of ....
33. 'How are you?' 'Very ...., thanks.'
34. The opposite of *beginning*.
35. The opposite of *come*.
37. You can see with this.
40. This is a good thing to do with food.
41. What colour .... your girlfriend's hair?
43. If you're not 33 across, you might have to go to this place.
46. A colour.
47. 'I'm tired.' '................ am I.'
50. The same as 35 across.
51. Would you like .... come to a party?
52. Water below 0 degrees Celsius.
53. This person works in a 43 across.
55. A thousand thousand.
58. How long are you staying here ....?
59. Don't .... to lock the door when you go out.
60. .... to lock the door when you go out.
61. Not all birds can ....

DOWN

1. I was .... to hear that you got on well with your boss.
2. I'd like to make an .... to see Dr Carter.
3. I eat three times a ....
4. We're having the Directors' .... on Tuesday.
5. 35 across, 50 across and 32 down are all the ....
6. A woman's name.
7. In 1931–32, an American walked .... from California to Turkey.
9. Is service ....?
10. If you buy something from me, I .... it to you.
12. The past participle of *do*.
13. Could you fill up with petrol and check the ...., please?
15. I live .... the fifth floor.
17. Prices often rise, but they never ....
19. Not right.
20. If you have an ...., you might have to go to 43 across.
22. 'This is a really boring film.' 'I don't ....; I think it's very good.'
23. Half of half of half of eight.
27. My father .... speak six languages.
28. 'What does she do?' 'She's .... economist.'
30. It's a .... to work for her.
32. The same as 50 across.
36. This is round.
38. When I was a child we were very poor. We all lived in one ....
39. You .... meet a tall dark stranger.
42. You can do this with your 37 across.
44. He was born in London 35 years ....
45. Sorry I'm late. Have you been waiting ....?
48. Coffee .... tea?
49. That man.
53. I neither like .... dislike this music.
54. The same as 42 down.
56. Not 33 across.
57. 'Sue's had a baby.' 'A girl .... a boy?'

25 From tree to paper

1 Put in the correct verb forms.

1. Postmen and postwomen, police officers, judges and Members of Parliament are .... by the government, from our taxes. (*pay*)
2. A lot of modern medicines are .... from plants that grow in the tropical rain forests. (*make*)
3. Most bread in England is now .... by large industrial bakeries. (*produce*)
4. Some of America's coal is .... by women – but none of Britain's is. (*mine*)
5. Rice is not .... everywhere in China, only in places where it is hot and wet. (*grow*)
6. There is a small factory near our house where microlight aircraft are .... (*build*)
7. In my son's school, children are .... by a different teacher for each subject. (*teach*)
8. Great numbers of birds are .... from Gibraltar every year, as they pass by on their migrations. (*see*)
9. Do you think that a lot of medicine is .... to people who don't need it? (*give*)
10. Where are stamps .... in your country? (*sell*)

2 Grammar revision. Put in *the* if necessary.

1. Our house was built in ...the... fifteenth century.
2. ...–... paper is made from .... wood.
3. It was invented by .... Chinese.
4. You can travel to .... United States by .... air or by .... sea.
5. Could you answer .... telephone? I'm busy.
6. .... iron is not so strong as .... steel.
7. 'Do you like this song?' '................. words are stupid, but I like .... music.'
8. 'Would you like a glass of wine?' 'No, thanks, I don't drink .... alcohol.'
9. Could you tell me .... way to .... nearest police station?

3 Write sentences to say what countries these languages are spoken in. Example:

French is spoken in France, Belgium, ...

| Japanese | Chinese | Arabic | German |
| English | Spanish | Russian | Greek |

4 Read the first text with a dictionary. Then fill in the blanks in the second text with words from the first.

SOME OF BRITAIN'S IMPORTS AND EXPORTS

Britain imports petroleum, mainly from the Middle East and Libya; cars from Europe and Japan; lamb and butter from New Zealand; and fruit from the EEC, South America and Africa.

Some of Britain's exports are: chemicals, which are produced all over the country; chocolate and sugar confectionery, which are made mostly in York and the South West; drinks, which are produced mainly in Scotland; and metals and metal products, which are manufactured in many regions including Yorkshire, South Wales, the Midlands and the Northern Region.

SOME OF AUSTRALIA'S IMPORTS AND EXPORTS

Australia .....1..... books from Britain, electronic equipment .....2..... Japan, ...3..... cars and heavy machines .....4..... Britain and the USA. Some of Australia's exports are: wool, ...5..... is produced .....6..... in the dry regions and .....7..... New South Wales; wheat, which .....8..... grown in .....9..... South East and in the region of Perth; sugar, which is .....10..... mainly in Queensland; and minerals (lead, zinc, etc.) which .....11..... imported .....12..... by Britain and Japan.

---

5 If you have Student's Cassette B, find Lesson 25, Exercise 2 (only the first six sentences are recorded here). Listen, and try to write down all the sentences.

6 Write about three things that are grown or manufactured or produced in your country; add as many details as you can.

SOON TO BE MADE INTO A MAJOR NOVEL

Nick

26 Who? What? Where?...

1 Put the correct form of the verb in each blank.

1. Last Saturday I was .... to Cambridge to visit a friend, and my wife wanted .... to Reading to run in a marathon. (*go; go*)
2. I telephoned the railway station .... what times the trains were. (*find out*)
3. I was .... that the 8.14 train would get me to London in time to reach Cambridge by 10.30. (*tell*)
4. So my wife drove me to the station on her way to Reading, and I was .... on the platform at 8.05. (*stand*)
5. A few minutes later, it was .... that the train was .... to be late. (*announce; go*)
6. I knew I was .... to miss my connection in London; but I couldn't phone my friend to tell him because the telephone on the platform was .... (*go; break*)
7. Meanwhile, my wife was .... other problems: there were road works on the way to Reading, and the main road was .... (*have; close*)
8. After a while she realised that she was lost; she was afraid she was going .... late. (*be*)
9. But she finally .... the sports ground. The gate was .... and there was a big sign saying 'Reading Harriers 2nd Annual Marathon – Sunday August 27th'. (*find; lock*)
10. Some days it's a mistake to get out of bed, as my mother used .... (*say*)

2 Look at these examples:

The Pastoral Symphony was written **by** Beethoven. (= Beethoven wrote it.)
The Pastoral Symphony was written **with** a pen made from a feather. (= Beethoven used a pen made from a feather to write it.)
Beethoven's foot was injured **by** a falling stone. (The stone fell by itself.)

Now put *by* or *with* in each sentence.

1. This land was taken from the Apaches .... the white people.
2. Some oriental rugs are made .... very young children.
3. Hollandaise sauce should always be stirred .... a wooden spoon.
4. This letter was written .... a left-handed person.
5. He was knocked down .... a flower pot that fell out of a seventh-floor window.
6. He was hit on the head and face .... a broken chair leg.
7. The cheese was covered .... a damp cloth.
8. I have been asked .... the Prime Minister to make no announcement until we have further information.

3 Complete the text with words from the box. Use a dictionary.

| built | rebuilt | repaired | added | damaged |
| used | burnt down | | | |

Glastrop Cathedral was founded by Henry Morcam in 1442, and was ....1.... between 1443 and 1458. During the Civil War it was ....2.... as a military headquarters, and was badly ....3.... It was ....4.... and restored after the war by Lord Evelyn Fairfax, and a new tower was ....5.... In 1824 part of the Cathedral was ....6....; it was not ....7.... until 1883.

Now read these notes and write a text about the house.

Stroud House: built James Stroud 1676
18th century used as farmhouse
damaged by fire 1776
bought Andrew Scott
repaired, new floor added
badly damaged in World War II
bought National Trust after war
completely rebuilt
opened to public 1968

4 Put one of the expressions from the box in each blank.

have a talk	have breakfast	have a look
have a dream	have a wonderful time	
have a shower	have a drink	have a baby

1. I'm sure you'll .... in Corsica; we've been there three times and enjoyed it every time.
2. What time do you usually ....?
3. Have you heard the news? Ellen and Jim are going to ....! I'm going to be a grandmother!
4. Sit down and .... while I finish this, and then we can talk.
5. I'm going to have to .... with Brian – I think he's been using our phone to call Australia.
6. I .... sometimes that I'm locked in a small room.
7. I'm so hot and tired! I think I'll .... before I start dinner, if you don't mind.
8. I think I heard the doorbell ring – could you ....?

Now put *have* into the correct tense.

9. Can I phone you back? We .... lunch right now.
10. I .... a conversation with Alison this morning when Jerry came into her office.
11. I .... a day off next Friday, so I'll try to finish this by Thursday.
12. We .... trouble starting the car when it's cold.

5 Revision. Complete the table of irregular verbs. Learn the ones you don't know.

INFINITIVE	PAST TENSE	PAST PARTICIPLE
speak	....	....
spell	....	....
spend	....	....
stand	....	....
swim	....	....
take	....	....
teach	....	....
tell	....	....
think	....	....
understand	....	....
wear	....	....
win	....	....
write	....	....

6 In a race, the results were as follows:

James beat Olson.
Olson was beaten by Andrews.
Peters was beaten by George and James.
Peters beat Smith.
Andrews was beaten by George, who was beaten by James.
Andrews beat Peters, and so did Olson.

Who won?

(*Solution on page 116.*)

---

27 Probability

1 Put in *will, might, can't* or *must*.

1. Next Monday .... be my 30th birthday.
2. I .... go to Spain next week, but I'm not sure yet.
3. 'Isn't that Joan over there?' 'No, it .... be her – Joan's much taller than that.'
4. There's somebody at the door. Do you think it .... be the postman?
5. 'I've been travelling since four o'clock.' 'You .... be tired.'
6. We haven't made definite plans for our holiday yet. We .... go to Greece or Italy, or we .... even stay at home.
7. This .... be John's coat. There's a letter addressed to him in the pocket.
8. 'I'm getting married next week.' 'You .... mean it!' 'I do.'

2 Is it true? You can use your dictionary. Use one of the expressions in the box to write what you think about each statement.

It must be true.   It's probably true.
It could be true.   It might be true.
It's probably not true.   It can't be true.

---

1. Some early skis have been found which are at least 4,500 years old.
2. A long time ago, mountains in Norway, Scotland, Greenland and the north-east US belonged to the same mountain chain.
3. When powerful people choose people to work with them, they usually choose people who will lie to them about how well things are going.
4. There is a fish that is more poisonous than any poisonous snake.
5. Some animals living very deep in the ocean can 'see' the extremely hot water that comes up from the ocean floor.
6. Our ideas about what makes a person good-looking depend partly on what country we grew up in.
7. In 1988, the greatest physicist in the world was a man who could not write, or even speak clearly.
8. Most algebra problems cannot be solved.
9. We will never be able to predict the weather accurately for longer than a few days.

(*Answers on page 116.*)

3 What did they say? Rewrite the sentences as in the example.

Dolores Ibarruri: 'It is better to die on your feet than to live on your knees!'

Dolores Ibarruri said that it was better to die on your feet than to live on your knees.

1. Virginia Woolf: 'The eyes of others are our prisons; their thoughts are our cages.'
2. Texas Guinan: 'Success has killed more men than bullets.'
3. Eleanor Roosevelt: 'No one can make you feel inferior without your consent.'
4. Mae West: 'Between two evils, I always pick the one I've never tried before.' Also: 'Too much of a good thing can be wonderful.'
5. Dodie Smith: 'Noble deeds and hot baths are the best cures for depression.'
6. Adele Davis: 'Thousands upon thousands of persons have studied disease; almost no one has studied health.'
7. Mother Teresa: 'Our work brings people face to face with love.'

4 Here are some of the questions from Fred and Janet's first conversation from the recording for the Student's Book. Rewrite them as in the example.

Fred: 'What's your name?'

Fred asked Janet what her name was.

1. Janet: 'What do you do, Fred?'
2. Janet: 'Where do you work?'
3. Janet: 'Are you based in London?'
4. Janet: 'Have I really (got an interesting face)?'
5. Fred: 'Are you an actress?'
6. Janet: 'You've got a Boeing 747?'
7. Janet: 'What does your father do?'

5 If you have Student's Cassette B, find Lesson 27, Exercise 1 (only the first part of the conversation is recorded here). Listen, and write down everything you hear.

6 Write answers to the questions.

1. What have people said to you that was not true? Write three things. (For example, *When I was small, my brother told me that babies were brought by rabbits.*)
2. Think of three questions you have asked people in the last few days and write them down. (For example, *I asked my English teacher if she spoke any other languages.*)
3. Is there a God? Why? Begin *There must/may/can't be a God, because . . .*

"Hold this for a moment, he said – and I haven't seen him since."

28 Somebody with blue eyes

1 Study the examples, and then decide where to put *both* in each sentence.

ONE-PART VERBS
We **both speak** Chinese.
My sister and I **both like** music.

TWO-PART VERBS
We **were both born** in September.
They **have both studied** in the USA.
Anne and Peter **can both sing** very well.

ARE/WERE
We **are both** fair-haired.
The two children **were both** very hungry.

1. My parents work in the same bank.
2. When I arrived, they were cooking.
3. You look like your mother.
4. Our children are tall and slim.
5. We have been in hospital recently.
6. The cars cost a fortune.
7. Alice and Judy can play chess.
8. I think those trees are going to die.

2 Do you remember how to write plurals?
Write the plurals of these words.

boy	way	coach
watch	lorry	difference
lady	reason	party
box	body	tomato
gun	valley	economy
day	switch	church
potato		

Do you remember the plurals of these words?
Look them up in your dictionary if you are not sure.

child	person	woman
wife	knife	foot

3 Where are they made? Example:

Wine is made in France, Spain, Australia, ...

jap

perfume   cars   cameras

calculators   cheese   wine   shoes

4 Spelling: double letters and single letters. Put another letter in where necessary. Examples:

thin̲ning   look̲ing

slim...er	short...er	prof...es...ion	qual...if...ications
at...ractive	fair-hair...ed	ed...ucation	program...e
wor...ied	depres...ed	hap...en...ed	show...ed
ner...vous	dif...er...ent	wal...et	sit...ing

57

5 Copy the text, choosing the correct verb forms.

Yesterday the doorbell (*was ringing / rang*) while I (*was having / had*) breakfast. As I (*was going / went*) to answer it, I (*was falling / fell*) over a pile of books in the hall. By the time I (*was getting / got*) to the door, there was no one there – but the postman (*was getting / got*) back into his van a few houses away. I (*was running / ran*) after him, but he (*wasn't hearing / didn't hear*) me and (*was driving / drove*) off. So I (*was going / went*) back home. When I (*was getting / got*) there, the door was shut, and I (*was realising / realised*) that I didn't have my key. My son was in the house, and so I (*was ringing / rang*) the bell, but he (*wasn't answering / didn't answer*): he (*was listening / listened*) to music and (*wasn't hearing / didn't hear*) the bell. I (*was remembering / remembered*) that the kitchen window was open, so I (*was going / went*) round to the back to try and get in that way. While I (*was climbing / climbed*) in the window, the electricity man (*was arriving / arrived*) to read the meter, and I had to explain the situation to him. I still don't know if he (*was believing / believed*) me. Anyway, I (*was getting / got*) in, only to find that the cats (*were eating / ate*) my breakfast. Then the doorbell (*was ringing / rang*).

6 Read the description of the first woman. Write a description from the notes about the second woman. Describe the third woman.

Carolyn   Ruth   Deborah

CAROLYN
Carolyn is a tall dark-haired woman in her late thirties. She is very pretty, with an oval face, beautiful fair skin and very light blue eyes. Her hair is straight and quite short. She is rather plump, but she dresses very attractively. She usually looks quite cheerful in a quiet way. She looks like a person who is easy to talk to.

RUTH
short, black, early twenties
quite plain, but very interesting
   face
hair: short, curly, black
eyes: big, brown
nose: small
face: round
skin: very dark
slim, athletic-looking
dresses casually
looks friendly and enthusiastic

"My God! I've got last year's body!"

"Got any S shirts?"

29 Things

1 **Singular countable noun, plural countable noun or uncountable noun? Complete the lists.**

shirt eye hair ear-rings ears jeans
wool glasses water watch apple beer
snow foot bank money feet pounds

SINGULAR COUNTABLE: shirt......

PLURAL COUNTABLE: ear-rings......

UNCOUNTABLE: water......

2 **Answer some of these questions using *too*. Use a dictionary if necessary. Example:**

Why can't you pick up a car? *Because a car's too heavy.*

1. Why can't a knife cut a stone?
2. Why can't you jump over a house?
3. Why can't you throw a fridge?
4. Why can't you sunbathe at the North Pole?
5. Why can't you put a horse in your bath?
6. Why can't you hear your heart beating?
7. Why can't you drink boiling water?
8. Why can't you read in the middle of a wood at midnight?
9. Why can't you jump across the Mississippi?
10. Why can't you eat rice before it's cooked?
11. Why can't you stand up in a car?

Now answer some of the questions using *enough*. Example:

Why can't you pick up a car? *Because I'm not strong enough.*

3 **Can you see something made of wood; something made of plastic; something made of metal; something made of rubber; something made of paper; something made of stone; something made of glass? Find the names of the things in a dictionary if necessary and write them down. Example:**

Made of wood: a door; the floor.

4 **Where are the stresses? Example:**

plastic

business cotton dictionary direct discover
education information invent liquid metal
narrow necessary photograph photographer
profession programme qualification something
surprised synthetic useful wonderful

5 **Choose three of the things in the box and write five sentences to describe each one. Example:**

A TYPEWRITER
A typewriter is a thing that you write with. It is made of metal and plastic. It is bigger than a watch but not as big as a car. It is quite heavy. Some typewriters are electric.

a fridge	a bath	a car	a computer
a wine bottle	a piano	a telephone	a yacht
a radio	a house		

6 **This is part of a real conversation between people who were playing 'Twenty questions'. Read the conversation and decide what the first speaker was thinking of – a flower, a glass, a typewriter, a guitar, a car key, a cat, a tin-opener, a stamp or an electric coffee-grinder.**

'I'll start if you like.'
'OK.'
'You've got to tell us whether it's animal, vegetable or mineral.'
'I have to tell you?'
'Yes.'
'You don't have to ask me?'
'No, you have to tell us that and then we have to ask the rest.'
'OK. It's mineral.'
'Is it manufactured?'
'Yes.'
'Is it smaller than a loaf of bread?'
'Yes.'
'Can you burn it?'
'It wouldn't burn well, no.'
'Is it something to do with the hospital?'
'No, not necessarily.'
'Does it have moving parts?'
'Not usually. No, it doesn't.'
'Is it useful?'
'Yes.'
'In the home?'
'Yes.'
'Can you eat it?'
'No.'
'Is it a kitchen utensil?'
'I wouldn't call it a utensil.'
'Have you got one in your house?'
'Yes.'
'More than one?'
'More than one.'
'More than ten?'
'More than ten.'
'Does it always come in a group – '
'No.'
'Anything to do with electrics?'
'No.'
'Are there any on this table?'
'Yes.'
'Is it a ....?'
'Yes.'
'I knew it was a .... from the very beginning.'

30 Self and others

1 Six people from different countries are in the same compartment on a long train journey. They would like to talk to each other. The table shows the languages that they speak. Write sentences to show how different people can talk to each other. Examples:

Alicia and Shu Fang can talk to each other in Spanish.
Alicia and Yasuko can talk to each other if Shu Fang interprets for them.

	English	French	Chinese	Japanese	Spanish	German	Swahili	Arabic	Russian
Alicia		✓			✓				
Shu Fang			✓		✓				
John	✓						✓	✓	
Yasuko	✓		✓	✓					
Mohammed Ali						✓		✓	
Erika	✓	✓				✓			✓

2 Do you do these things yourself, or does somebody else do them for you? Examples:

I repair my car myself.
Somebody else washes my clothes.

1. repair your car/motorbike/bicycle
2. wash your clothes
3. clean your house/flat/room
4. answer your letters
5. make your bed
6. iron your clothes
7. buy your food
8. cook your food
9. buy your clothes

3 Invent ends for these sentences.

1. Parents should . . .
2. Children should . . .
3. Teachers should . . .
4. Politicians should . . .
5. Everybody should . . .
6. I should . . .

"It's not the fighting I hate, it's the washing-up!"

"I'm sure you and mother will like each other."

4 Write out the letter, putting punctuation and capital letters where they belong.

14 september 1990

dear kevin

im writing to ask you for some advice   barbara and i are getting very worried about richard   he has been staying out very late at night and is always too tired to do well in school   last week he was out till one in the morning on tuesday and wednesday   he wont listen to anything we say   we have tried not giving him pocket money but it doesnt do any good   i am afraid that now he is sure that we are just trying to make him do what we want to show him whos boss but the truth is   we are worried about his future

i know you and simon had a rough patch when he was sixteen or so   what did you do about it   how did you handle it   any advice you could give us would be very welcome   we have run out of ideas ourselves

sorry to write such a short letter but i want to get this in the post today   give my love to angela and the kids

yours

tony

5 Write an answer to the letter in Exercise 4. Or write a letter giving advice to somebody you know (a real person).

6 Read this with a dictionary.

WHAT A BLESSING YOUNGER BROTHERS ARE
When my sister says to me,
'Go and put the kettle on,'
I say to my younger brother,
'Go and put the kettle on,'
So my brother goes and puts the kettle on.
When my younger brother says to me,
'Bring a tin of fruit up,'
I say to my elder sister,
'Bring a tin of fruit up,'
But she says,
'Go yourself you lazy thing,'
So I say to my younger brother,
'Go yourself you lazy thing!'
So he goes and brings the tin of fruit up.

(Catherine Frankland, aged 13)

you have to love your own baby because everyone else finds them a newsance.

(Patrick, aged 8)

'Newsance': nuisance – something irritating

I know my mother and father love each other because my mother cooks him his favorite roast every night

(Theresa, aged 8)

My budgie broke is neck because he was always kissing himself in the mirrer.

(Tim, aged 6)

love is important becaus if people did not love each other there wouldn't be any people.

(Lynn, aged 7)

Summary **E**

1 Write sentences to say what these things are made of. Use a dictionary if necessary.

I think the boot is made of plastic.

2 Put in *me, you, him, her* etc.; *myself, yourself, himself, herself* etc.; *each other*; *somebody else*.

1. 'Mary's going to marry a Japanese.' 'Good heavens! How will they understand ....?'
2. I often talk to .... when I'm alone.
3. 'I don't like these flowers.' 'Well, give them to ....' 'Who?' '...............'
4. 'Why are you walking like that?' 'I hurt .... playing football.'
5. 'Who went with ....?' 'Nobody. She went by ....'
6. Stop looking at .... in the mirror – you're not as beautiful as all that.
7. 'Who does the cleaning for old Mrs Collins?' 'Nobody. She does it ....'
8. Little Joe is only two, but he can dress ....
9. He never listens to ...., and she never listens to ....

4 Do you prefer to do these things by yourself or with somebody else?

listen to music   go to the cinema
go shopping   go on holiday
have lunch   go for a walk

What other things do you prefer to do by yourself or with somebody else?

3 Match the nouns and the adjectives. Use a dictionary if necessary.

disco music   a diamond   hard   soft   strong
helium   lightning   a whale   loud   quiet   big
lead   a mouse   Superman   small   wide   narrow
a tortoise   an atom   butter   tall   light   heavy
the Amazon   the Bering Strait   fast   slow
a Californian redwood tree

62

5 Translate these into your language.

1. Most paper is made from wood.
2. English is spoken here.
3. He asked me where I worked.
4. It must be true.
5. It can't be true.
6. Children should do some of the housework themselves.
7. Do you think that people who are in love should tell each other everything?
8. They're talking about themselves.
9. They're talking about each other.
10. He's not going to marry Judy; he's fallen in love with somebody else.
11. We both read the newspaper every day.
12. Neither of us has got a cat.

6 Here is some of the vocabulary from Lesson 30. Write a short story using at least ten of the words and expressions – more if you can.

housework; clean; cook; decorate; iron; mend; shop; wash; wash up; employ; think about; look at; feel sorry for; visit; photograph; fall in love with; marry; hurt; choose; teach; learn; free; married; honest; somebody else; each other.

"All right – what have the Wright-Pattersons got now?"

"Hello, George – remember you said that although I was going to marry Martin James you'd always be waiting for me if ever I should change my mind?"

"Mr Jepson said that while I was sending out for coffee he would like a hamburger. Mr Willis said that he thought he would like a hamburger, too, medium with no tomato. Ms Lester said that that sounded good and that she would like a hamburger, too, rare with a side of French fries. Mr Anderson said that if everybody else was going to have something to eat he might as well have a meatball sandwich and a piece of apple pie. Mrs Colby said she'd like a slice of anchovy pizza and a bag of Fritolays . . ."

"We have a description, sir: the grey-blue eyes were steady but cold, the mouth hard and cruel with an arrogant curl to the upper lip, while the deep lines running from the almost Roman nose to frame the wilful chin spoke of selfishness and passion."

Revision E

1 Match the beginnings and the ends of the definitions.

An American is   a place where you can watch films.
A match is   a person who comes from America.
A cinema is   a thing that you light a cigarette with.
A chair is   a piece of furniture for sitting on.
Breakfast is   getting from a lower place to a higher place.
Water is   a meal that you eat in the morning.
Climbing is   something you wash yourself in.

Now choose ten or more of these and write definitions for them.

a businessman	an office	a lighter
a guitar	juice	a cheque
a motorbike	paper	returning
a butcher	a key	phoning someone
hair	a passport	lunch
a neck	a camp site	a customer
a hat	sugar	tea
a neighbour	a canteen	a map
stealing	preferring	a dentist
a nose	a car	medicine
a cafe	a lorry	spelling
pepper	a cassette	a driver
a jacket	an ear	a mirror
refusing	a disco	milk

2 Look at this example.

a book

Is it animal, vegetable or mineral?
It's vegetable and mineral

Is it alive?
No, it isn't

Is it useful?
Yes, it is

Now answer these questions.

a leather handbag

1. Is it animal, vegetable or mineral?
2. Is it alive?
3. Can you eat it?
4. Is it made of wool?
5. Is it useful?
6. Can you find it in a kitchen?
7. Is it liquid?
8. Is it very heavy?
9. Is it soft?
10. Is it manufactured?
11. Have you got one of these?
12. Can you see one now?
13. Do most people have one?
14. Can you put things in it?
15. Is it made of plastic?
16. Can you open and close it?

3 If you have Student's Cassette B, find Revision Lesson E, Listening Exercise 1 (only the first speaker is recorded here). Look up the words in the box in your dictionary. Then listen to the recording and try to write it all down.

rationalise   aware

"Don't ask me – I thought they were yours."

64

4 Read the text with a dictionary.

IRON AND STEEL

Copper and tin were used before iron: they melt at a lower temperature, and can be mixed to form a useful metal called bronze.

Iron was probably first extracted from meteorites, perhaps around 3000 BC. (Iron ornaments dating from 5,000 years ago have been found in the Middle East.) Later, iron was extracted from iron ore (impure iron) by the Hittites, around 2000 BC. The iron was first heated, then hammered to remove the impurities, then cooled. Finally, the iron was heated again and shaped into tools or weapons.

Later, in India first of all, people found out how to make fires hot enough to melt iron (at a temperature of 1,539°C), by driving air through the fuel. This made it possible to produce steel. Steel is made from iron mixed with a little carbon (0.15%–0.25%). Steel is harder than pure iron, and is less brittle (it does not break as easily). Every motorist is the owner of a ton of steel.

Now put these in the correct order.

a. Hotter fires became possible.
b. People got iron from meteorites.
c. Steel was produced.
d. Bronze was first made.
e. People hit heated ore to get iron.

5 Try to remember a phone conversation that you have had recently. Write about 100 words to report what was said.

6 Try the crossword.

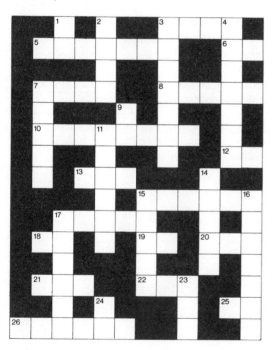

15. I'm .... the doctor about my leg tomorrow.
17. Opposite of *heavy*.
18. It's a quarter .... four.
19. Do you mind .... I call you Mike?
20. Be careful! I .... my finger on that knife yesterday.
21. How long .... did you start working here?
22. Opposite of *high*.
25. I'm seeing her .... Tuesday.
26. Could I .... your pen for a minute?

DOWN

1. 'Where's John, do you know?' '................ was here a minute ago.'
2. I didn't sleep well last night – the bed in the hotel was too ....
3. Some shoes are made of ....
4. Could you speak a little louder? I can't hear you – they're .... and playing loud music upstairs.
7. Keys are made of ....
9. 'Where's the front door key?' 'I left .... on the table.'
11. Is the room warm .... for you?
14. Her family has been in the village .... 1726.
15. It's very late – is Bernard .... at the office?
16. It's .... colder: I think it will snow tonight.
17. The new car is .... than the old one, so it's more difficult to park.
23. '................ didn't Janice come?' 'I don't think she was invited.'
24. Debbie wasn't home, ... I left a message with her daughter.

(*Solution on page 116.*)

ACROSS

3. Opposite of *quiet*.
5. 'Why can't you come to the party?' '................ it's my best friend's birthday, and I'm taking him to dinner.'
6. His sister's .... architect.
7. Do you .... if I smoke?
8. I've been to America .... : once in 1982 and once last year.
10. Judy and I live in the same street, so we drive to work ....
12. Did you .... to Barry's yesterday?
13. I've known her .... twelve years now.

31 Before and after

1 Look at the examples and then join the sentences together in the same way.

I have breakfast. Then I get dressed. (*before*)

I have breakfast before I get dressed

I go to bed. Then I read for a bit. (*after*)

I read for a bit after I go to bed

1. I brush my teeth. Then I undress. (*before*)
2. I get into bed. Then I put the light out. (*after*)
3. I wake up. Then I get up. (*as soon as*)
4. I met Jane. Then my life changed. (*after*)
5. She was very unhappy. Then she left school. (*until*)
6. I thought I was very ill. Then I went to see the doctor. (*before*)
7. I telephoned Kate. Then I went to see her. (*before*)
8. I went to America. Then everything got better. (*after*)

2 Which happened first?

1. Before I went to France, I studied French for six months.

   First I studied French. Then I went to France.

2. After I left school, I made a lot of new friends.
3. Before I went out, I cleaned my shoes.
4. After you came to see me, I felt fine.
5. Before Andrew got to London, it started raining.
6. After it got dark, Paul went out for a walk.
7. Before I took off the handbrake, I looked in the mirror.
8. Just after your mother telephoned, your father came to see me.

3 Put in *still, yet* or *already*.

1. 'Haven't you finished ....?'
2. 'No, I'm .... working.'
3. 'When's Mary coming?' 'She's .... here.'
4. 'Are you ready?' 'No, I haven't done my packing ....'
5. Ann's doing very well at school. She's .... got a university place, and she's only sixteen.
6. 'What's the weather like?' 'It's .... raining.'
7. 'Is it lunchtime?' 'Not ....'
8. 'Have you phoned Godfrey ....?' 'No, I'm going to do it this evening.'
9. Look at the time! It's .... eight o'clock. We really must go.

4 If you have Student's Cassette B, find Lesson 31, Exercise 6 (only the first part of the conversation is recorded here). Listen and write down what you hear.

5 Put in *such* or *so*.

1. His letter was .... rude that I didn't know how to answer.
2. Ann's friends are .... strange!
3. I didn't know you had .... a big house.
4. I'm .... tired that I think I'm going to bed.
5. It was .... a slow train that it would have been faster to walk.
6. I've never met .... kind people as your family.
7. I didn't expect it to be .... cold – I wish I'd brought my coat.
8. It's been .... terrible weather that the farmers haven't been able to grow anything.

"Let's get this straight, Simpson – after you had a bath, which plug did you pull out?"

6 See how much of this story you can understand *without* using a dictionary. Then choose *only* five words to look up in the dictionary and read it again.

THE LITTLE GIRL AND THE WOLF
One afternoon a big wolf waited in a dark forest for a little girl to come along carrying a basket of food to her grandmother. Finally a little girl did come along and she was carrying a basket of food. 'Are you carrying that basket to your grandmother?' asked the wolf. The little girl said yes, she was. So the wolf asked her where her grandmother lived and the little girl told him and he disappeared into the wood.

When the little girl opened the door of her grandmother's house she saw that there was somebody in bed with a nightcap and nightgown on. She had approached no nearer than twenty-five feet from the bed when she saw that it was not her grandmother but the wolf, for even in a nightcap a wolf does not look any more like your grandmother than the Metro-Goldwyn lion looks like the President of the United States. So the little girl took an automatic pistol out of her basket and shot the wolf dead.

Moral: It is not so easy to fool little girls nowadays as it used to be.

(from *The Thurber Carnival* – adapted)

32 I hadn't seen her for a long time

1 Can you write the names of the cardinal and ordinal numbers?

1 one....... first.......

1	11	21
2	12	30
3	13	100
4	14	1,000
5	15	
6	16	
7	17	
8	18	
9	19	
10	20	

2 Can you pronounce these words with the right stress? Look in your dictionary or vocabulary index if you are not sure.

afternoon   cinema   difficult   directions
examine   family   goodbye   language
realise   recognition   repair   reserve
restaurant   silence   someone   suitcase

3 Can you complete the list?

January, February, . . .

Do you know the days of the week?

1. What is the day after Thursday?
2. What is the day before the day before Tuesday?
3. What is the day after the day before Sunday?
4. What is today?
5. What was the day before yesterday?
6. What is the day after tomorrow?
7. What day is your birthday on this year?

4 If you have Student's Cassette B, find Lesson 32, Exercise 2. Listen to the song and write down one or more verses.

5 Read the text (use a dictionary for the most difficult words). Some of the words have been left out: you will find them in the box. Write the correct word for each blank.

| and but had has have shall was were |

Crazy bank machine pays £195 jackpot

Police ......1...... last night investigating the mystery of a mad money machine which handed out a jackpot payment to a week-end shopper.

Brewery worker Mr David Baker tapped out a request for £15 on a National Westminster Bank cash dispenser at Kingston, Surrey, and ......2...... rewarded with about £195 in crisp fivers.

At their home in Kingston his wife, Mrs Deborah Baker, 30, said: 'He immediately handed the money over to the police. He ......3...... quite astonished.

'Some of the money obviously belonged to the lady who ......4...... used the machine before him. She ......5...... wanted £50 and got nothing.

'The machine ......6...... obviously gone up the wall. My husband handed over the £50 to the lady behind him, ...7...... he was still left with quite a lot of money.'

A spokesman for National Westminster said: 'Luckily there ......8...... a member of the staff nearby ......9...... the machine ......10...... switched off.

'I just do not know what made it go berserk. It is a normally reliable machine. We ......11...... make a thorough investigation.'

At Kingston police station a spokesman said: 'We have had a number of complaints about the machine. I sent a young special constable down to investigate but I ......12...... not heard from him for some time – perhaps he ......13...... gone to the South of France . . .'

(Sunday Express)

6 Imagine that you are David Baker. Write the story of what happened to you when you went to get money from the National Westminster Bank cash dispenser.

33 All right, I suppose so

1 Complete the sentences with question tags.

1. You're not going to invite him, *are you* ?
2. She's very late, ...
3. He doesn't like pop music, *isn't it*
4. The meeting's on Tuesday, ...
5. You haven't got £5 on you, ...
6. We'll have to hurry, ...
7. You won't be late home tonight, ...

8. Ann was away yesterday, ...
9. She can't swim, ...
10. You like Bach, *don't you*
11. Your mother isn't religious, *is she*
12. You'd like a drink, ...
13. John wasn't at the party, *was he*
14. You went to school in Scotland, *didn't you*
15. Mary doesn't know I'm here, *does she*

2 What do these road signs tell you to do or not to do? Examples:

Sign A tells you to turn left.
Sign B tells you not to park.

not to overtake – уступи дорогу

 A B C STOP D E

F G 30 H I J

not to ride a bicycle

3 Some of these words are stressed on the first syllable (like *carpet*), and some are stressed on the second syllable (like *invite*). Divide them into two groups, according to the stress, and then practise pronouncing them. Use a dictionary to help you if necessary.

about   afraid   afterwards   already   carpet   difference   directions
everybody   exactly   forget   happen   invite   language   manager   promise
remember   repair   restaurant   secretary   silence   somebody   suppose

68

4 Complete the dialogue with the words and expressions from the box.

afraid	been trying	been waiting
by	for	goes	have to	have to
if	me to	month	must	must
to	urgent	us to	won't	you to

MR L: Er, Miss Collins.

MISS C: Yes, Mr Lewis?

MR L: I'd like ......1...... do a couple of letters for me, ...2...... you don't mind.

MISS C: Well, er, Mr Martin has just asked ......3...... do a letter for him. He says it's ......4......

MR L: Well, I'm ......5...... he'll ......6...... wait. I've ......7...... to get these letters written all week, and they ......8...... go today. I ......9...... keep you long.

MISS C: Right, Mr Lewis.

MR L: This letter is ......10...... John Barlow, at Barlow and Fletcher, in Manchester.

'Dear Mr Barlow

Thank you for your letter of April 14, in which you ask ......11...... wait a further six weeks for delivery of our order. I am afraid that this is out of the question. We have already ......12...... eight weeks ......13...... these urgently needed parts, and we ......14...... have them by the end of the ......15...... If they do not arrive ......16...... April 30, I regret to say that we shall ......17...... cancel the order and look elsewhere.

Yours sincerely

Paul Lewis.'

See that this ......18...... today, Miss Collins, would you?

MISS C: Yes, of course, Mr Lewis.

MR L: And now a letter to . . .

5 If you have Student's Cassette B, find Lesson 33, Exercise 1. Listen and imitate the pronunciation. Pay special attention to intonation (the musical rise and fall of the voice).

6 Read this with a dictionary. Can you write some misleading advice for foreign visitors to your country?

Misleading advice for foreigners

[The *New Statesman* magazine set a competition in which readers were asked to give misleading advice to tourists visiting England for the first time. These are some of the entries.]

Women are not allowed upstairs on buses; if you see a woman there, ask her politely to descend.

Visitors in London hotels are expected by the management to hang the bedlinen out of the windows to air.

Try the famous echo in the British Museum Reading Room.

On first entering an underground train, it is customary to shake hands with every passenger.

If you take a taxi, the driver will be only too willing to give your shoes a polish while waiting at the traffic-lights.

Never attempt to tip a taxi-driver.

Public conveniences are few; unfrequented streets where relief is permitted are marked 'P'.

Parking is permitted in the grounds of Buckingham Palace on payment of a small fee to the sentry.

Never pay the price demanded for a newspaper; good-natured haggling is customary.

public conveniences: public lavatories
unfrequented: deserted
sentry: soldier on guard
haggling: arguing about the price

"I must warn you, Miss Pringle, there's an awful lot of paperwork."

"Remember me from last night?"

34 If he had been bad at maths, . . .

1 Write a past conditional sentence for each situation.

1. Yesterday began as a terrible day for Chris. He didn't hear the alarm clock, so he got up late.

   If he had heard the alarm clock, he would have got up on time.

2. He usually reads the paper in the morning, but he didn't yesterday.

   He would have read the paper if he hadn't got up late.

3. He was really late, so he decided to drive instead of taking the bus.
4. He was worried about being late, and he didn't close the house door (properly).
5. He saw it was open, and got out of the car to close it.
6. In his hurry, he locked the car with the keys inside.
7. He ran back into the house to get the other car keys, and knocked a jar of jam all over the kitchen.
8. The main road to his office was closed for repairs – it had been in the paper that morning, but he hadn't read the paper.
9. When he finally got to work, he was really late, and there were no more places in his office car park.
10. He spent twenty minutes looking for a parking place. He should have taken the bus!
11. His boss thought he was ill and gave some of his work to his colleague Janice.
12. When he walked into the office, the boss gave him a new project, working with a firm of architects.
13. He was surprised to find out that the receptionist at the architects' was an old school friend that he hadn't seen for years; he was delighted that the boss hadn't given the job to someone else.
14. The boss said she had meant to give the project to Janice, but gave it to Chris because Janice had already started on his old project.

3 *The woman's arm wouldn't have been burnt if the car hadn't crashed.* Make some more sentences about what wouldn't have happened.

4 Pronunciation. Say these sentences with the right stress.

1. If she'd been **bad** at **lang**uages, she would have **stud**ied **maths**.
2. She'd have be**come** a **teach**er if she'd **stud**ied **maths**.
3. If she **hadn't** de**cid**ed to be**come** an **in**terpreter, she'd have **gone** to **teach**er **train**ing **college**.
4. If she'd **gone** to **teach**er **train**ing **college**, she would have **met** Alice **there**.
5. She **wouldn't** have **met** An**drew** if she'd **gone** to **teach**er **train**ing **college**.
6. If she **hadn't met** An**drew**, she **wouldn't** have **gone** to **Crete**.

2 Put a word from the box into each blank in the text. You can use your dictionary.

adopt	animal	angry	arm	car	fish	fish	injured
local	lost	love	oil	phoned	police	put	turn

Expensive kindness

A West German woman's ......1...... for cats has brought her an ......2...... cat and a bill for £23,000.

The story, told by German ......3......, began when the 56-year-old woman from Wuppertal ......4...... her cat and ......5...... an advertisement in the ......6...... paper.

A man ......7...... her to say he had found the ......8......, but in fact it was not hers. However, she felt sorry for the cat, which must have been a stray, and decided to ......9...... it.

On the way home in her Mercedes ......10......, the cat 'suddenly went wild' and bit and scratched her ......11....... This caused the car to ......12...... off the road and crash into a parked car, bringing down a sausage stand and a neighbouring ......13...... and chip stand.

Boiling ......14...... burnt the arms of a 44-year-old woman selling ......15...... and chips, and a 21-year-old woman who was waiting for her chips fainted and ......16...... herself falling to the pavement.

(adapted from an article by Anna Tomforde in the *Guardian*)

70

5 Vocabulary revision and extension. Label the pictures; you can use a dictionary. Then complete the vocabulary networks (you will not use all the words). (Answers on page 117.)

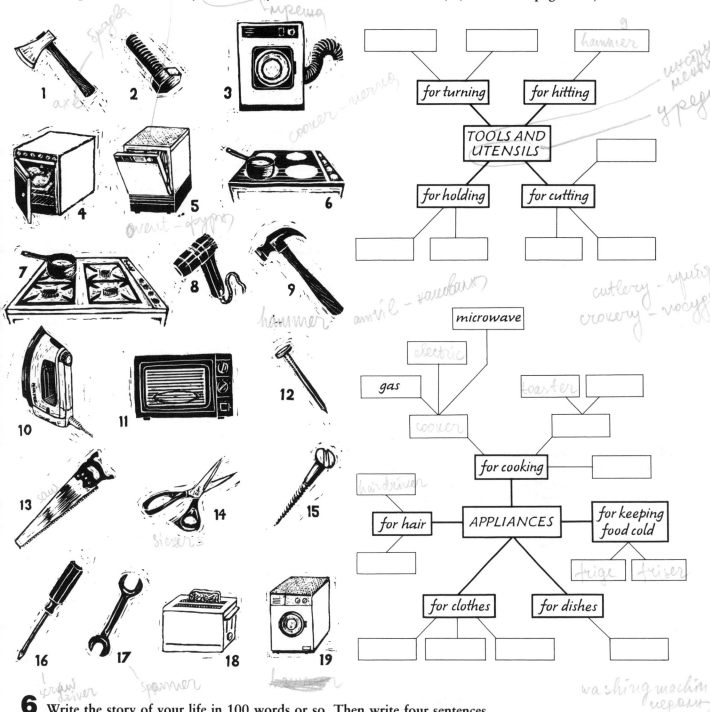

6 Write the story of your life in 100 words or so. Then write four sentences about it using 'If . . . had(n't) . . . , . . . '

---

35 Travel

1 You can go to a travel agent's to make enquiries about a holiday, to buy an air ticket to New York, because you want to make a reservation on a train, and for lots of other reasons. You can go to a petrol station to buy petrol, to have the oil checked, because the petrol pump attendant is a friend of yours, etc. Why did you last go to the following places (answer with *To . . .* or *Because . . .*):

a petrol station; a travel agent's; an airport; a bus stop; a garage;
a station enquiry office; a police station; a post office; a bank.

2 Put in the right 'question tags'.

1. It's a nice day, isn't it ?
2. You look very like your father, ...
3. You aren't tired, ...
4. Mary doesn't drink wine, ...
5. Your mother speaks Chinese, ...
6. The garden's looking nice, ...
7. People are all different, ...
8. You've got a cold, ...
9. He doesn't drive very well, ...
10. You want to speak to the manager, ...

3 Put in *anybody, somebody, nobody, everybody, anything, something, nothing* or *everything*.

1. I think there's .... at the door.
2. I'm sorry – I haven't got .... for you to drink.
3. I think you know .... who's here, don't you?
4. ....'s worrying me – can I talk to you about it?
5. .... really knows what goes on inside children's heads.
6. Has .... seen Janet today?
7. She had her bag stolen in London: she lost her passport, her money, her air ticket – ....
8. 'Would you like a sandwich?'   'No, ... to eat, thank you.'

4 If you have Student's Cassette B, find Lesson 35, Exercise 2. Choose three or more of the pieces of conversation and try to write down the words. Turn to Practice Book page 117 to check your answers.

5 Imagine you are standing outside the main post office in a city or town in your country. Somebody asks you the way to a bank, or a railway station, or a museum, or somewhere else (you decide exactly where). Write what you will say to him or her.

6 *Strange but true!* Read this with a dictionary.

The scientist Thomas Young could read when he was two years old, and had read the Bible twice when he was four. He learnt twelve languages as a child, and could play a large number of musical instruments.

By the age of thirteen, the French linguist Champollion had learnt Latin, Greek, Hebrew, Arabic, Syrian, Chaldean and Coptic. When he was 21 he solved the mystery of ancient Egyptian hieroglyphic writing.

Sir John Bowring (1792–1872) was said to be able to read 200 languages and speak 100. The New Zealander Dr Harold Whitmore Williams could communicate in 52 languages, and was fluent in 28.

500 years ago Leonardo de Vinci produced designs for a parachute, a life jacket, a water pump, a paddle boat, a steam gun, a lens-grinding machine, a machine gun, a helicopter, a submarine, and a number of other modern inventions. He was also one of the greatest artists that has ever lived.

The American chess master Morphy once played eight games of chess simultaneously while blindfolded. (He won six of the games.)

"What about my exhaust, officer?"

"George, is there a mountain near here?"

36 Shall I open it for you?

1 Look at the picture. Where are things? Where should they be? Example:

There's a chair on the piano.
It should be on the floor.

2 Put in prepositions or adverb particles from the box.

at	away	back	down	for	on	off
out	out of	to	up			

1. Look ....*at*.... my new shoes!
2. I've lost my keys. Can you help me look ....*for*.... them?
3. It's getting dark. Shall I switch ....*on*.... the light?
4. Would you like to take ....*off*.... your coat and sit ....*down*....?
5. Let's listen ....*to*.... some music.
6. Could you pick ....*up*.... the children's shoes and put them ....*away*....?
7. This meat's bad. I'll have to take it ....*back*.....
8. Tell Ann to put ....*on*.... her coat before she goes ....*out*.....
9. 'What's the weather like?' 'Why don't you look ....*out of*.... the window?'
10. 'Here's your shopping.' 'Thanks – just put it ....*up*.... over there.'

3 Complete the table.

WHO?	WHO(M)?	WHOSE?	WHOSE?	–
I	me	my	mine	myself
you	....	....	....	....
he	him	....	....	....
she	....	....	....	....
it	....	its	–	itself
we	....	....	....	....
you	....	....	....	....
they	....	....	....	....

4 Vocabulary revision and extension. Match the words and the numbers.

carpet   ceiling   cupboard   door   floor
garden   gate   light   roof   shelf   sink
tap   wall   washbasin   window

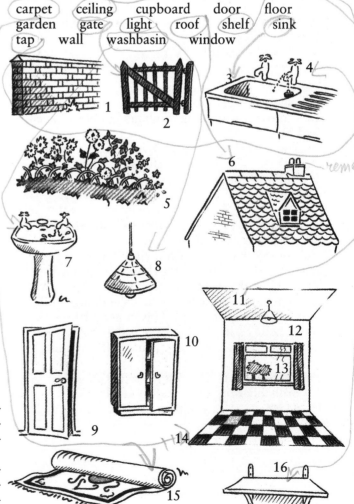

73

5 Practise saying these words with the correct stress.

afterwards   **along**   **careful**   **cross**roads
everybody   ex**act**ly   **fin**ally   for**get**
handbag   in**vite**   **man**ager   **mid**night
per**mission**   **prom**ise   **rail**way   re**mem**ber
secretary   sup**pose**

6 Imagine an English friend is coming to visit you in your home. Write a letter, giving precise instructions on how to drive to your home from the main road into your city/town/village.

"I am standing under your foot."

Summary F

1 Make questions.

1. Gloria gets up very early. (*What time . . . ?*)
2. The church was built by Wren. (*When . . . ?*)
3. I'm waiting. (*What . . . for?*)
4. He was sacked last week. (*Why . . . ?*)
5. We're going on holiday in June. (*Where . . . ?*)
6. I don't usually sit here. (*Where . . . ?*)
7. He never travels by car. (*How . . . ?*)
8. My father was killed when I was six. (*How . . . ?*)

2 Put in words from the box.

already	back	believe	boss		months
must	news	nice	remember		same
see	still	work	yet		

'Hello, Pam. Any ....1.... of Jane?'
'Well, she's ....2.... from holiday.'
'Yes, I know. I was going to phone her but I haven't had time ....3....'
'You know, she's ....4.... in love with that student.'
'What, the ....5.... one that she was in love with last month? Hasn't she got tired of him ....6....?'
'That's not a very ....7.... thing to say, Mary.'
'Well, she's ....8.... been in love three times this year to my certain knowledge, and it's only March.'
'Jane's a warm-hearted girl.'
'You can say that again, Pam. How's her ....9.... going? Is she ....10.... with Universal Sprockets?'
'Yes, ...11.... there. That makes two ....12.... now.'
'That ....13.... be a record. How's she doing?'
'Pretty well. They've ....14.... given her a rise.'
'I don't ....15.... it. She can't spell, she can't type, she can't ....16.... her own name half the time.'
'I think the ....17.... fancies her.'
'That ....18.... be it. OK, Pam, I've got to go. I'll probably drop in at the weekend, OK?'
'OK, Mary. ....19.... you then. Bye.'
'Bye.'

3 Make sentences with the Present Perfect Progressive tense.

1. How long | you | wait?

   How long have you been waiting?
2. I | try | to phone him all day.
3. We | live | in this house for about twelve years.
4. Janet | practise | the violin all afternoon.
5. I | wait | for a letter from my father for weeks.
6. How long | you | learn | English?
7. People | fight | each other for millions of years.
8. They | talk | for a long time.
9. It | rain | since I got up this morning.

4 Translate these into your language.

1. I hadn't seen her since the day we said goodbye.
2. When I got back to the table she had gone.
3. If his parents had been well off, he would have gone to university.
4. 'You're French, aren't you?' 'No, I'm Swiss.'
5. He asked her if he could have a party.
6. She told him to tidy up afterwards.
7. Would you like me to switch the lights on?
8. John's still in bed. He hasn't woken up yet.
9. Susan is already dressed.
10. 'Shall I open it for you?' 'No, thanks. I can do it myself.'
11. I'll answer the door, shall I?
12. 'Would you like to dance?' 'I'd love to.'

5 Here is a story called *The Medical Book*. Put the pictures in the right order, and then write the story of what happened. Use some of the words in the box.

after	after that	before	finally	next	then	until	when

6 Write about a time when you went to see the doctor or went to hospital.

"Let's see, now – I'm sure we can fit you in somewhere."

"You booked us a holiday abroad during the summer. Could you tell us, please, where we went?"

Revision F

1 Vocabulary revision and extension. Can you match the pictures and the games?

badminton   baseball   basketball   bowling
cricket   football   ice-hockey   rugby
snooker   table tennis   tennis

2 Put in *there is/are, there was/were, there has/have been, there will be* or *there would be.*

1. Do you think .... people on other planets?
2. I don't think .... ever .... so many people unemployed.
3. .... sunshine in most parts of the country tomorrow.
4. When I got to Anne's place .... two police cars outside.
5. I don't believe that .... life after death.
6. .... a phone call for you last night.
7. Hello. Is that the police? .... an accident in Station Road.
8. If people behaved sensibly, ... no more wars.

3 Write suitable answers to these offers.

1. Shall I make some coffee?
2. Would you like to go and see a film?
3. Would you like to dance?
4. Can I take your coat?
5. Would you like me to put the lights on?
6. I'll close the door, shall I?

4 If you have Student's Cassette B, find Revision Lesson F, Listening Exercise 2. Listen to the song and write down the verbs. Check on Student's Book page 125.

5 Read this with a dictionary.

SEAGULL

What does a seagull
know about being a seagull?
What does it feel
as it hangs above the cliff edge
adjusting its wings to the wind,
turning its bright yellow eye
this way and that?

Watching it hover
then fall away sideways
and, gathering speed,
glide so effortlessly down
to a gleaming wet rock,
we are moved by its movement.
We feel it like music.

But what of the seagull?

(*Bob Rogers*)

"Just think, I'd have been an old man by now if I'd ever grown up."

6 Try the crossword.

[crossword grid]

ACROSS

1. You put a letter in it.
4. Have you got some .... for cleaning windows?
8. I usually .... up at 6.30.
9. I usually wait until my hair is too long before I go to the ....
14. You can use this for frying.
15. I am.
16. The opposite of *false*.
17. Can you .... this letter into French for me?
20. Would you prefer tea .... coffee?
21. I first met her ten years ....
22. And we're .... friends after all this time.
24. He's been looking for a .... since he left school, and he still hasn't found one.
27. Could you pick .... those bits of paper?
28. 'Good music.' 'I don't .... I think it's terrible.'
29. You can fly in this.
30. The opposite of *beginning*.
31. Elephants eat grass and leaves, don't .... ?

DOWN

1. Four twos.
2. Value Added Tax (*abbreviation*).
3. You use this to hear with.
5. Union of Soviet Socialist Republics (*abbreviation*).
6. Money you pay to travel.
7. Between your wrist and your shoulder.
9. Not hers.
10. Not .... birds can fly.
11. The last thing you will do.
12. Keep .... on until you get to a crossroads and then turn right.
13. France and Poland are in .... , but Nigeria and Japan are not.
14. 'Shall I take your coat?' 'No thanks, I'll keep it ....'
18. Like a mouse, but bigger.
19. I'll tell you as soon .... possible.
22. Stuff to wash with.
23. If you don't know a word, you can .... it up in a dictionary.
24. The month before the month after the month before July.
25. Shall I .... the door for you?
26. You can do this in *29 across*.

(*Solution on page 117.*)

"About what time does the 9.20 leave?"

"Was the train very crowded, dear?"

Mini-grammar

Special verbs: *be* and *have* (*got*)

Be

Present tense		
I am (I'm)	am I?	I am not (I'm not)
you are (you're)	are you?	you are not (you're not / you aren't)
he is (he's)	is he?	he is not (he's not / he isn't)
she is (she's)	is she?	she is not (she's not / she isn't)
it is (it's)	is it?	it is not (it's not / it isn't)
we are (we're)	are we?	we are not (we're not / we aren't)
you are (you're)	are you?	you are not (you're not / you aren't)
they are (they're)	are they?	they are not (they're not / they aren't)

I'm from India.
I'm sixteen. (I have sixteen.)
'**Are** you English?' 'Yes, I **am**.' ('Yes, I'm.')
Her name**'s** Ann.
'**Is** Susan an engineer?' 'Yes, she **is**.' ('Yes, she's.')
Are your brothers at school? (Are at school your brothers?)

Past tense		
I was	was I?	I was not (wasn't)
you were	were you?	you were not (weren't)
he/she/it was	was she *etc.*?	he *etc.* was not (wasn't)
we were	were we?	we were not (weren't)
you were	were you?	you were not (weren't)
they were	were they?	they were not (weren't)

'When you **were** a small child, **were** you happy?'
'Yes, I **was**.' 'No, I **wasn't**.'
Were your parents poor? (Were poor your parents?)
We **weren't** poor, but we **weren't** rich.

Stress and pronunciation

I was /wəz/ hungry. Yes, I was /wɒz/.
I **wasn't** /wɒznt/ happy.
We were /wə/ poor. Yes, we **were** /wɜː/.
We **weren't** /wɜːnt/ happy.

Present Perfect and Future

I **have been** ill for the last few weeks.
Where **has** John **been** all day?

Tomorrow **will be** cold and wet.
I**'ll be** back home about six o'clock.

There is

Present and past tenses		
there is (there's) there are	is there? are there?	there is not (isn't) there are not (aren't)
there was there were	was there? were there?	there was not (wasn't) there were not (weren't)

Stress and pronunciation

There's a **big** table in my kitchen. (/ðəzə/)
Is there any **milk** in the **fridge**? (/ɪz ðər 'eni/)
Yes, there **is**. (/ðər 'ɪz/)
No, there **isn't**. (/ðər 'ɪznt/)
There are some **apples**. (/ðər ə səm/)
Are there any **oranges**? (/'ɑː ðər 'eni/)
Yes, there **are**. (/ðər 'ɑː/)
No, there **aren't**. (/ðər 'ɑːnt/)
There was some **coffee** on the table. (/ðə wəz səm/)
There **wasn't** any **ice** in her **glass**. (/ðə 'wɒznt/)
There **weren't** any potatoes. (/ðə 'wɜːnt/)

Present Perfect and Future

There **has been** an accident.
Have there **been** any phone calls for me?

There **will be** snow at the weekend.
There **won't be** a meeting tomorrow.

Have (got)

Have got (possession, relationships, etc.)

Present tense		
I have (I've) got you have (you've) got he *etc.* has (he's) got we have (we've) got you have (you've) got they have (they've) got	have I got? have you got? has she *etc.* got? have we got? have you got? have they got?	I have not (haven't) got you have not (haven't) got he *etc.* has not (hasn't) got we have not (haven't) got you have not (haven't) got they have not (haven't) got

You've **got** beautiful eyes.
'**Have** you **got** any sisters or brothers?'
'Yes, I **have**. I've **got** two sisters.'   'No, I **haven't**.'
'**Has** your mother **got** any sisters?' ('~~Has got your mother any sisters?~~')
'Yes, she **has**. She's **got** two.'   'No, she **hasn't**.'
We've **got** a new car.
They **haven't got** any money.

1. *Have got* means the same as *have*; we use them both to talk about possession and relationships. British people prefer *have got* when they speak and write informally. Americans more often use *have* without *got*.
2. With *had*, we do not use *got* so often. We often use *did* to make past questions and negatives (see below).
3. *Have* can also mean *eat*, *take*, etc. (see below). With these meanings, we do not use *got*, and we use *do* to make questions and negatives.
4. We also use *have* to make the perfect tenses of other verbs (see below). We do not use *got* or *do* in this case.

Have (= *eat*, *take*, etc.)

Present tense		
I have you have he/she/it has we have you have they have	do I have? do you have? does he/she/it have? do we have? do you have? do they have?	I do not (don't) have you do not (don't) have he/she/it does not (doesn't) have we do not (don't) have you do not (don't) have they do not (don't) have

What time **do** you **have** breakfast?
She always **has** a bath in the morning.
Have a good holiday.

The past of *have got* and *have*

I had you had he/she/it had we had you had they had	did I have? did you have? did he/she/it have? did we have? did you have? did they have?	I did not (didn't) have you did not (didn't) have he/she/it did not (didn't) have we did not (didn't) have you did not (didn't) have they did not (didn't) have

When she was young she **had** long fair hair.
We **didn't have** a car when I was a child.
We **had** a wonderful holiday last summer.
What time **did** you **have** breakfast this morning?

Present Perfect and Future

I **have had** a lot of problems this year.
How long **have** you **had** that car?

I think I'll **have** a bath now.
I don't know if we **will have** time to see your mother.

Have and *be*

We use *be*, not *have*, with *hungry*, *thirsty*, *hot*, *warm* and *cold*; and to talk about age, size and colour.

I'm hungry. (~~I have hungry.~~)
Are you thirsty? (~~Have you . . . ?~~)
If you're cold, put a sweater on.

He's 27. (~~He has 27.~~)
What size **are** your shoes?
What colour **is** her new car?

Ordinary verbs: present tenses

Simple Present

I work	do I work?	I do not (don't) work
you work	do you work?	you do not (don't) work
he/she/it work**s**	do**es** he *etc.* work?	she *etc.* do**es** not (doe**sn**'t) work
we work	do we work?	we do not (don't) work
you work	do you work?	you do not (don't) work
they work	do they work?	they do not (don't) work

I **live** in Curzon Street.
'**Do** you **like** orange juice?'   'Yes, I **do**.'   (~~'Yes, I like.'~~)
What time **does** Karen **get** up?
. (~~. . . does Karen gets . . .~~)
'**Does** she **go** to work by car?'   'No, she **doesn't**.'
My father **doesn't work** on Mondays.
   (~~. . . doesn't works . . .~~)
'**Do** Sam and Virginia **live** near you?'   'No, they **don't**.'

Stress and pronunciation

'**Do** you (/dju:/) **like** orange **juice**?'
'Yes, I **do**.'   'No, I **don't**.'
What time does (/dəz/) **Karen get up**?
'**Does** (/dəz/) she **have breakfast**?'
'Yes, she **does** (/dʌz/).'   'No, she **doesn't** (/'dʌznt/).'

Spelling of *he/she/it* forms

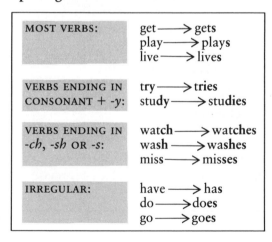

MOST VERBS:	get ⟶ gets play ⟶ plays live ⟶ lives
VERBS ENDING IN CONSONANT + -y:	try ⟶ tries study ⟶ studies
VERBS ENDING IN -*ch*, -*sh* OR -*s*:	watch ⟶ watches wash ⟶ washes miss ⟶ misses
IRREGULAR:	have ⟶ has do ⟶ does go ⟶ goes

Pronunciation of *he/she/it* forms

1. /z/ after vowels and most voiced sounds (/b/, /d/, /g/, /v/, /ð/, /l/, /m/, /n/, /ŋ/)

   goes /gəʊz/   sees /si:z/   stands /stændz/
   lives /lɪvz/   tells /telz/   runs /rʌnz/

2. /s/ after most unvoiced sounds (/p/, /t/, /k/, /f/, /θ/)

   stops /stɒps/   starts /stɑːts/   looks /lʊks/

3. /ɪz/ after /s/, /z/, /ʃ/, /ʒ/, /tʃ/, /dʒ/

   presses /'presɪz/   uses /'ju:zɪz/   pushes /'pʊʃɪz/
   watches /'wɒtʃɪz/

Present Progressive

I am (I'm) looking	am I looking?	I am not (I'm not) looking
you are (you're) looking	are you looking?	you are not (you're not / you aren't) looking
he/she/it is (he's *etc.*) looking	is she *etc.* looking?	he *etc.* is not (he's not / he isn't) looking
we are (we're) looking	are we looking?	we are not (we're not / we aren't) looking
you are (you're) looking	are you looking?	you are not (you're not / you aren't) looking
they are (they're) looking	are they looking?	they are not (they're not / they aren't) looking

I'm **looking** for a blue sweater.
Everybody **is looking** up. (~~Everybody are . . .~~)
They **are wearing** green suits.
'**Is** the commentator **looking**?' ('~~Is looking the commentator?~~')
'Yes, he **is**.' 'No, he **isn't**.'
What **is** the woman in the red dress **doing**? (~~What is doing the woman . . .~~)
I'**m not** working today.
The price of bread **is going** up.
People **are getting** taller.
What **are** you **doing** tomorrow?

Non-progressive verbs

With some verbs (for example *know, want, like, remember, have* meaning 'possess', *be*), we usually use simple tenses, not progressive tenses.

I **know** who she is. (~~I am knowing . . .~~)
Do you **want** to go home now? (~~Are you wanting . . . ?~~)
I **don't like** this music. (~~I'm not liking . . .~~)
She **has** (got) a headache. (~~She is having . . .~~)

Spelling of *-ing* forms

MOST VERBS:	work ⟶ working eat ⟶ eating
VERBS ENDING IN *-e*:	make ⟶ making (~~makeing~~) write ⟶ writing
SHORT VERBS ENDING IN ONE VOWEL + ONE CONSONANT:	stop ⟶ stopping sit ⟶ sitting run ⟶ running
VERBS ENDING IN *-ie*:	lie ⟶ lying die ⟶ dying

The difference between the two present tenses

1. We use the Simple Present to talk about:

– things that are true all the time

The earth **goes** round the sun.
Water **boils** at 100° Celsius.
I **speak** French.

– things that happen often, usually, sometimes *etc.*

I usually **study** from five to seven o'clock.
Helen often **wears** red.

2. We use the Present Progressive to talk about:

– things that are happening or changing now, these days

The water'**s boiling**. I'll make coffee.
I'**m studying** very hard just now.
Look. Helen'**s wearing** a lovely red dress.
The price of bread **is going** up.
People **are getting** taller.

– plans for the future (see below, page 86)

We'**re going** to Ann and Peter's for Christmas.
What **are** you **doing** tomorrow?

Telling stories with present tenses

One day, Anna **is walking** in the park when a man **stops** her. It **is** Boris. He **tells** her . . .

Ordinary verbs: past and perfect tenses

Regular and irregular past tenses and past participles

INFINITIVE	PAST TENSE	PAST PARTICIPLE
Regular verbs		
work	worked	worked
play	played	played
live	lived	lived
stop	stopped	stopped
try	tried	tried
etc.		
Irregular verbs		
be	was/were	been
come	came	come
go	went	been/gone
know	knew	known
learn	learnt	learnt
see	saw	seen
etc.		

(For a complete list of irregular verbs in *The New Cambridge English Course* Levels 1 and 2, see Student's Book 2 page 128.)

Simple Past

I stopped	did I stop?	I did not (didn't) stop
you stopped	did you stop?	you did not (didn't) stop
he/she/it stopped	did she *etc.* stop?	he *etc.* did not (didn't) stop
we stopped	did we stop?	we did not (didn't) stop
you stopped	did you stop?	you did not (didn't) stop
they stopped	did they stop?	they did not (didn't) stop

She **left** Lima by air.
How far **did** she **fall**? (~~. . . did she fell?~~)
She **did** not **recognise** the people. (~~. . . did not recognised . . .~~)
'**Did** you **like** school when you were a child?'
'Yes, I **did**.' ('~~Yes, I liked.~~')

Spelling of regular past tenses

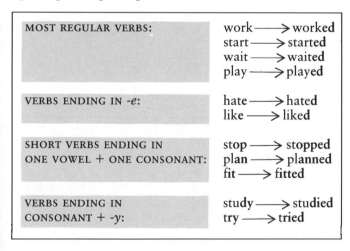

MOST REGULAR VERBS:	work ⟶ worked
	start ⟶ started
	wait ⟶ waited
	play ⟶ played
VERBS ENDING IN -*e*:	hate ⟶ hated
	like ⟶ liked
SHORT VERBS ENDING IN ONE VOWEL + ONE CONSONANT:	stop ⟶ stopped
	plan ⟶ planned
	fit ⟶ fitted
VERBS ENDING IN CONSONANT + -*y*:	study ⟶ studied
	try ⟶ tried

Pronunciation of regular past tenses

1. /d/ after vowels and voiced sounds (/b/, /g/, /v/, /ð/, /l/, /z/, /ʒ/, /dʒ/, /m/, /n/, /ŋ/)

   agreed /əˈgriːd/   played /pleɪd/   lived /lɪvd/
   pulled /pʊld/   used /juːzd/

2. /t/ after /p/, /k/, /f/, /θ/, /s/, /ʃ/, /tʃ/

   stopped /stɒpt/   worked /wɜːkt/
   watched /wɒtʃt/

3. /ɪd/ after /t/ and /d/

   started /ˈstɑːtɪd/   decided /dɪˈsaɪdɪd/

Past Progressive

I was trying you were trying he/she/it was trying we were trying you were trying they were trying	was I trying? were you trying? *etc.*	I was not (wasn't) trying you were not (weren't) trying *etc.*

We use the Past Progressive for 'background' events – to say what was going on at a particular time, or at the moment when something happened. We use the Simple Past for a shorter event which came in the middle of the 'background' event, or which interrupted it.

What **were** you **doing**
—✗—
at 7.15
last night?

I **was getting** ready to come home
—✗—
and the
phone **rang**.

Just when I **was trying** to finish some work
—✗—
Janet
turned up.

The TV
broke down
—✗—
while we **were watching** the news.

Simple Present Perfect

(*have* + past participle)		
I have (I've) seen you have (you've) seen he *etc.* has (he's) seen we have (we've) seen you have (you've) seen they have (they've) seen	have I seen? have you seen? has she *etc.* seen? have we seen? have you seen? have they seen?	I have not (haven't) seen you have not (haven't) seen he *etc.* has not (hasn't) seen we have not (haven't) seen you have not (haven't) seen they have not (haven't) seen

Ways of using the Simple Present Perfect

– Talking about experience

'**Have** you ever **eaten** snails?'
'Yes, I **have**.'
'No, I **haven't**.'
'No, I never **have**.'

– Giving news

Fantasia **has signed** a treaty with Outland.
The River Fant **has** just **burst** its banks.
I've lost my keys – could you help me look for them?

– Talking about changes (differences between past and present)

The population of Fantasia **has increased** since 1950.
The percentage of homeless people **has fallen**.
She **has got** much fatter during the last few years.

Simple Present Perfect and Simple Past with time expressions

1. We use the Present Perfect:
   – when we are thinking of a period of time that is not finished (for example *this week/month/year, since . . .*)
   – when we mean 'at any time up to now' (for example, with *ever, never, before*)

   I've changed my job three times **this year**.
   (I changed my job three times . . .)
   Have you **seen** Carmen **before**?
   (Did you see Carmen before?)
   Have you **ever been** to America?
   She **has never learnt** to drive.

2. We use the Simple Past:
   – when we are thinking of a period of time that is finished (for example with *ago, yesterday, last week/month/year* etc., *then, when*)

   I changed my job **last week**.
   (I have changed my job last week.)
   I **saw** Carmen three years ago.
   (I have seen Carmen three years ago.)
   (. . . ago three years . . . before three years)
   Did you **go** to California **last summer**?
   She **learnt** to fly **when** she was 18.

Present Perfect Progressive

I have (I've) been working you have (you've) been working *etc.*	have I been working? have you been working? *etc.*	I have not (haven't) been working you have not (haven't) been working *etc.*

Using the Present Perfect Progressive

We use the Present Perfect Progressive to say that something started in the past and is still happening (or has only just finished). We often use the Present Perfect Progressive to say or ask *how long* something has been happening. We do *not* use a present tense to do this.

For the last six days he **has been visiting** Third World countries.
  (~~. . . he is visiting . . .~~)
Demonstrators **have been marching** through the centre for several hours.
Heavy rain **has been falling** steadily for the past four weeks.
Have you **been waiting** long? (~~Are you waiting long?~~)

Non-progressive verbs

With some verbs (for example *know, remember, want, have* meaning 'possess', *be*), we usually use simple tenses, not progressive tenses.

They **have known** each other for a long time.
  (~~They have been knowing . . .~~)
How long **have** you **had** that coat?
  (~~. . . have you been having . . .?~~)
I've **been** in this class since October.

The difference between the Present Perfect and the Present

To say *how long* something has been happening, use a Present Perfect tense, not a Present tense. Compare:

i **know** her well.
I **have known** her **since 1980.** (~~I know her since 1980.~~)

We **live** in Harwich.
We **have lived** here **for 10 years.** (~~We live here for 10 years.~~)

She **is** in the advanced class.
She's **been** in the class **for three weeks.** (~~She is . . .~~)

He **is studying** English.
He **has been studying** English for five years.
  (~~He is studying . . .~~)

For and *since*

For + period   = *since* + beginning of period.

for 24 hours   = since yesterday
for three days   = since Sunday
for ten years   = since we got married
for a long time = since the 15th century

I've been working **for twelve hours.**
  (~~I've been working since twelve hours.~~)
I've been working **since six a.m.**
  (~~I'm working since six a.m.~~)
We've lived here **for ten years.**
  (~~We've lived here since ten years.~~)
  (~~We live here for ten years.~~)
I've known her **since 1980.**
  (~~I know her . . .~~)

Past Perfect

I had (I'd) seen you had (you'd) seen *etc.*	had I seen? had you seen? *etc.*	I had not (hadn't) seen you had not (hadn't) seen *etc.*

The Past Perfect is a 'before-past': we use it to talk about a second, earlier past time.

BEFORE-PAST	PAST
She **had gone**	when **I got** back to the table.
I'd changed so much	she **didn't realise** it was me.

For the use of the Past Perfect in reported speech, see page 100.
For the use of the Past Perfect with *if*, see page 99.

Talking about the future

Present Progressive (plans)

Are you **doing** anything this evening?
I'm working on Thursday.
We're leaving for Cardiff on Monday.

Be going + infinitive (plans and predictions)

Plans

What **are** you **going to do** next year?
I'm **going to learn** Chinese.
We're going to take ten litres of water with us.

Predictions

We're going to crash!
It's going to rain.
She's going to have a baby.

Will (predictions *etc.*)

I/you/he/*etc.* will ('ll) go (~~I will to go~~   ~~he wills go~~) will I/*etc.* go? (~~do I will go?~~) I/*etc.* will not (won't) go

You **will** have a long and interesting life.
I hope my children **will** be good-looking.
They probably **won't** be tall.

Tomorrow **will be** warm and sunny.
If you don't eat you'**ll die**.

For *'ll* used for offers, see page 104.

Present Progressive, *going to* and *will*: the differences

1. Plans:
   We use both the Present Progressive and *going to* to talk about plans. We use the Present Progressive especially when we talk about times and places. Compare:

   I'm going to travel round the world.
   I'm travelling to France next week.

2. Predictions:
   We use both *going to* and *will* to predict (to say what we think or know will happen in the future). We prefer *going to* when we can 'see things coming' – when it is very clear what is going to happen. Compare:

   Look! **It's going to rain**.
   Perhaps it **will snow** tomorrow.

   She'**s going to have** a baby.
   Do you think the baby **will have** blue eyes?

Passives

Simple Present Passive

SUBJECT	AM/IS/ARE	PAST PARTICIPLE	
Most paper	is	made	from wood.
Trees	are	transported	to paper mills.

Simple Past Passive

SUBJECT	WAS/WERE	PAST PARTICIPLE	
The Taj Mahal	was	built	by Shah Jehan.
Hamlet	was	written	in about 1600.
The trees	were	blown down	by a big storm.

Active and passive

The Chinese **invented** paper.
Paper **was invented** by the Chinese.

Shakespeare **wrote** *Hamlet.*
Hamlet **was written** in 1600.

-ing form and past participle

She is **watching** TV.
That programme is **watched** by 30 million people every week.

When I went to see her she was **writing** letters.
Hamlet was **written** by Shakespeare.

Imperatives, infinitives and *-ing* forms

Imperatives

Examples: *run*; *tell*; *don't run*; *don't tell*

We use imperatives for giving advice and instructions.

Run early in the morning – it's better.
Meet me at seven o'clock.
Always wear comfortable clothing.
   (~~Wear always comfortable clothing.~~)
Never run in fog. (~~Run never in fog.~~)

Don't run if you've got a cold.
Don't tell Carola.

Infinitives with *to*

Examples: *to see*; *to go*

We use infinitives with *to*:

– after certain verbs (for example *hope, want, have, would like/love, try*)

  I **hope to see** you soon.
  I **don't want to go** home.
  You **have to change** at Coventry.
  '**Would** you **like to dance**?' 'I'd **love to**.'
  Let's **try to understand** each other.

– after *something, anything, nothing*

  Would you like **something to eat**?
  I haven't got **anything to wear**.
  There's **nothing to do**.

– after some adjectives

  This is **hard to understand**.
  She's very **nice to work** with.

– to say why we do things ('infinitive of purpose')

  'Why did you come here?' '**To see** you.'
    ('~~For see you.~~')
  You go to a supermarket **to buy** food.

Infinitives without *to*

Examples: *see*; *go*

We use infinitives without *to*:

— after *do*, and after modal verbs (*can, could, will, would, may, might, shall, should*, and *must*)

Why **don't** you **borrow** something of mine?
Can you **lend** me some stamps?
  (~~Can you to lend . . . ?~~)
Could you **speak** more slowly?
It **will rain** tomorrow.
What **would** you **like**?

— after *Let's*

Let's all **go** and see Ann.

— after *had better*

I'd better get moving.

— after *make* + object

This dress **makes me look** like a sack of
  potatoes.

-ing forms

Examples: *seeing*; *going*

We use *-ing* forms:

— after certain verbs (for example *like, love, hate*)

I **like speaking** French.
I **love going** to the theatre.

— in progressive tenses

'What are you **doing**?' 'I'm **writing** letters.'

— after all prepositions

Thank you **for coming**.
She's good **at swimming**.

Modal verbs

The grammar of modal verbs

Can, could, will, would, may, might, shall, should, must, and *ought* are
called 'modal verbs'. They are a special kind of auxiliary verb.

1. Modal verbs have no *-s* in the third-person
singular present.

   She **can** swim. (*NOT* ~~She cans swim.~~)
   It **may** rain tomorrow.

2. Modal verbs (except *ought*) are followed by the
infinitive without *to*.

   I **must go**. (~~I must to go.~~)
   Should I **phone** Ann?

3. Questions and negatives are made without *do*.

   Can you **speak** French?
     (~~Do you can speak French?~~)

4. Modal verbs have no infinitives or past participles.
We use other expressions instead.

   When will you **be able to** pay?
     (~~When will you can pay?~~)
   I've never **been able to** understand her.
     (~~I've never could . . .~~)
   You'll **have to** work harder next year.
     (~~You'll must . . .~~)

Meaning and use

Probability and certainty

It **must** be true.
It **may** be true.
It **could** be true.
It **might** be true.
It **can't** be true.

It **will** rain tomorrow.
It **might** snow, but it's not very likely.
If you go on this holiday, you **may** win $1,000,000.
You **would** feel much better if you went to bed.

Permission and obligation

Can I go home early today?
Excuse me. **Could** I speak to you for a moment?
  (More polite than *Can I . . . ?*)
You **can** borrow my coat if you like.
Applicants **must** be able to swim.
Children **should** do some of the housework themselves.
You **ought to** stop smoking.

Past permission and obligation

I **was allowed** to go home early yesterday.
  (~~I could . . .~~)
My father **had to** work very hard when he was young.
  (~~My father musted . . .~~)

Ability

I **can** sing.
I **can't** dance.
'**Can** you swim?' 'Yes, I **can**.'
Sorry, I **can't** see you tomorrow.
The government **cannot** please everybody.
  (NOTE: *cannot* is written as one word.)
I **could** swim very well when I was younger.
If I had more time I **could** learn another language.
  (= . . . I would be able to learn . . .)

Offering and asking

Can I help you?
Could you speak more slowly, please?
Shall I carry your bag?
Would you like a cup of tea?

Pronunciation: strong and weak forms

I can /kən/ swim, but I **can't** /kɑːnt/ dance.
Yes, I **can** /kæn/.
You must /məst/ try harder.
You **mustn't** /ˈmʌsnt/ say anything to Ann.
Yes, I **must** /mʌst/.

NOTE: *can't* is pronounced /kɑːnt/ in British English and /kænt/ in American English.

Had better and *used to*

These two expressions are used rather like modal verbs.

We use *had better* like *should*, to give advice (to other people or ourselves). The meaning is present, not past.

I'm late. **I'd better** go. (~~. . . I'd better to go.~~)
Somebody **had better** help Alice.
You'd better not tell anybody.

We use *used* + infinitive to talk about things that happened once, but do not happen now. There is no present *use to* . . . (We use the Simple Present instead.) *Did* can be used in questions and negatives.

I **used to be** very shy, but now I'm OK.
People **didn't use to travel** by car.
Did you **use to collect** stamps when you were younger?

Nouns and articles

Plurals of nouns

MOST NOUNS:	boy ⟶ boys girl ⟶ girls name ⟶ names parent ⟶ parents
NOUNS ENDING IN CONSONANT + -y:	family ⟶ families secretary ⟶ secretaries
NOUNS ENDING IN -ch, -sh, -s OR -x:	watch ⟶ watches crash ⟶ crashes address ⟶ addresses six ⟶ sixes
IRREGULAR:	child ⟶ children man ⟶ men woman ⟶ women life ⟶ lives wife ⟶ wives knife ⟶ knives foot ⟶ feet potato ⟶ potatoes tomato ⟶ tomatoes

Pronunciation of plural -s

1. /z/ after vowels and most voiced sounds (/b/, /d/, /g/, /v/, /ð/, /l/, /m/, /n/, /ŋ/)

   days /deɪz/   trees /triːz/   heads /hedz/
   wives /waɪvz/   miles /maɪlz/   pens /penz/

2. /s/ after most unvoiced sounds (/p/, /t/, /k/, /f/, /θ/)

   cups /kʌps/   plates /pleɪts/   books /bʊks/

3. /ɪz/ after /s/, /z/, /ʃ/, /ʒ/, /tʃ/, /dʒ/

   buses /ˈbʌsɪz/   noses /ˈnəʊzɪz/   watches /ˈwɒtʃɪz/

4. Exception: house /haʊs/ ⟶ houses /ˈhaʊzɪz/

Articles

A and an; pronunciation of the

We use *an* before vowels.

an artist   **an** engineer   **an** apple   **an** orange
an hour (/aʊə/)

We use *a* before consonants.

a doctor   **a** housewife   **a** banana   **a** tomato
a university (/juːnɪˈvɜːsəti/)

Before vowels, *the* is pronounced /ðiː/.

the egg /ðiː ˈeg/   the Italians /ðiː ɪˈtælɪənz/

Before consonants, *the* is pronounced /ðə/.

the book /ðə ˈbʊk/   the problem /ðə ˈprɒbləm/

A/an and the

We use *the* when the listener *knows which one* we are talking about.

Do you mind if I open **the window**? (*The listener knows which window.*)
Who's **the girl** in the red dress? (*I tell the listener which girl I mean.*)
We've got a cat and a dog. **The dog**'s name is Pete. (*The listener knows which dog I mean, because of the sentence before.*)

We use *a/an* when we mean 'any one', 'it doesn't matter which one', or when the listener doesn't know which one.

I'd like to have **a dog**.
She lives in **a small flat** somewhere in Paris.

And we use *a/an* when we give the class or group that somebody/something is in.

'What do you do?'   'I'm **a student**.' (~~'I'm student.'~~)
'What's that?'   'It's **a camera**.'

We also use *a/an* to mean 'every' in prices and measurements.

eighty pence **a** kilo   fifty kilometres **an** hour

Expressions without articles

at home (~~at the home~~)   go home (~~go to home~~)
in bed   at school   at work

Countable and uncountable nouns

The difference between countable and uncountable nouns

Countable nouns are the names of things that you can count. (For example: *a car, one* **problem**, *two* **trees**, *four hundred* **pounds**.) We can use *a/an* with countable nouns (*a/an* means 'one'). Countable nouns have plurals.

Uncountable nouns are the names of things that you can't count. (For example: *milk, air, music*: you can't normally say *two milks* or *four musics*.) Normally, we can't use *a/an* with uncountable nouns, and they have no plurals. Compare:

Would you like **a** sandwich?
Would you like **some** milk?
   (Would you like a milk?)

I like **those books**.
I like **that music**. (. . . those musics.)

Generalisations: not using *the*

When we talk about things in general (for example: *all oranges, all music* or *all oil*), we do not use *the* with plurals or uncountables.

Oranges were expensive when I was young.
   (The oranges . . . .)
I like **music**. (I like the music.)
Oil is produced in Texas.

We use *the* to talk about *particular things that the listener knows about.*

'Could you pass **the oranges**?'   'Here you are.'
The music's too loud. Could you turn it down?

Some problems with countables, uncountables, singulars and plurals

The following words are uncountable. We do not use them with *a/an*, and they have no plurals: *advice, information, hair, bread, news, weather, English* (and the names of other languages), *medicine, flu, toothache* (but *headache* is countable).

Could you give me **some information**?
   (. . . an information . . . some informations)
I'd like to give you **a piece of advice**.
   (. . . an advice.)
What colour **is** her **hair**?
Here **is** the **news**.
We're having terrible **weather**.
   (. . . a terrible weather.)
She speaks very good **English**.
   (. . . a very good English.)
I've got **toothache**. (*BUT* I've got **a headache**.)

Words like *pound, dollar, franc, yen, peseta* are countable, but the word *money* is uncountable.

It costs eight **francs**.
It costs a lot of **money**. (. . . a lot of moneys.)

Trousers, jeans, pyjamas, pants etc. are plural. So are *glasses* and *stairs*.

Those trousers are too big for you.
I need **some** new **jeans**. (. . . a new jean.)
I wear **glasses** for reading.
It's up the **stairs** on the right. (. . . the stair . . .)

A/an and *some/any*

We normally only use *a/an* with singular countable nouns. With plural and uncountable nouns *a/an* is not possible. We often use *some* and *any* (see below).

There's **a woman** at the reception desk.
There are **some books** on the table.
There's **some milk** in the fridge. (There's a milk . . . .)

Pronouns, determiners and question words

Subject and object pronouns

SUBJECT	OBJECT
I	me
you	you
he	him
she	her
it	it
we	us
you	you
they	them

He likes **me**, but I don't like **him**.
They've invited **us** to a party.
Could **you** give **me** some water?
'Who's that?' 'It's **me**.'
I'm taller than **her**.

Possessives

Possessive determiners and pronouns

DETERMINER	PRONOUN
my	mine
your	yours
his	his
her	hers
its	–
our	ours
your	yours
their	theirs

That's **my** bicycle over there. (~~. . . the my bicycle . . .~~)
Ann and **her** husband work in Stoke. (~~. . . his husband . . .~~)
John and **his** wife both play tennis. (~~. . . her wife . . .~~)
'Whose is that coat?' '**Mine**.'
Their house is bigger than **our** house, but I think **ours**
    is nicer than **theirs**.

Possessive 's

Singular: -'s
Plural: -s'

Sam is **Judy's** boyfriend. (~~. . . the Judy's boyfriend.~~)
Susan's surname is Perkins. (~~Surname's Susan . . .~~)
That's my **parents'** house.
All the **tourists'** suitcases got put on the wrong bus.

Pronunciation of possessive -s

AFTER A VOWEL:	/z/	Judy's Mary's Joe's Harry's
AFTER A VOICED CONSONANT:	/z/	Sam's Bob's Anne's Susan's
AFTER AN UNVOICED CONSONANT:	/s/	Eric's Margaret's Jeff's Kate's
AFTER /s/, /z/, /ʃ/, /ʒ/, /tʃ/, /dʒ/:	/ɪz/	Alice's Joyce's George's Des's

---

Reflexives, *each other* and *else*

Reflexive/emphatic pronouns

myself	ourselves
yourself	yourselves
himself	themselves
herself	
itself	

She's always talking to **herself**.
They only think about **themselves**.
I usually do my ironing **myself**.

Each other

People who love **each other** should try to be honest with
    each other. (~~People who love themselves . . .~~)

Somebody else

I didn't break the window – it was **somebody else**.
Do you usually go on holiday by yourself or with
    somebody else?

This, that, these, and *those*

This cheese is terrible.
These tomatoes are very nice.
How much is **that** sweater over there?
I like **those** ear-rings that she's wearing.

Some, any and *no*

Some and *any*

We usually use *some* in affirmative ('yes') sentences, and *any* in questions and negative ('no') sentences.

AFFIRMATIVE	QUESTION	NEGATIVE
There's **some** bread.	Is there **any** bread?	There isn't **any** bread.
I've got **some** eggs.	Have you got **any** eggs?	I haven't got **any** eggs.

Some in questions

When we offer things or ask for things, we usually use *some* in questions.

Would you like **some** coffee?
Could you lend me **some** sugar?

No (= *not any*)

I'm sorry, there's **no more** roast beef.
(= . . . there **isn't any** more . . .)

(NOTE: *No* and *not any* are negative, but *any* is not negative.)

I've got **no** friends = I haven't got **any** friends,
   NOT ~~I've got any friends.~~

Somebody, anything etc.

somebody	anybody	everybody	nobody
something	anything	everything	nothing
somewhere	anywhere	everywhere	nowhere

Somebody telephoned when you were out.
Would you like **something** to drink?
Have you got **anything** to read?
Have you seen my glasses **anywhere**?
I didn't understand **anything**.
Everybody was late.
She gave **everything** to her children.
'What are you doing?' '**Nothing**.'

Somebody etc. can be followed by adjectives.

I think she's **somebody important**.
Something very strange happened.
Did **anything interesting** happen?
Let's go **somewhere nice**.

Everybody, everything, nobody and *nothing* are singular.

Is everything all right? (~~Are everything . . . ?~~)
Everybody knows him.
Nobody likes him.

Quantifiers with uncountables and plurals

WITH UNCOUNTABLES	WITH PLURALS
(not) much	(not) many
how much?	how many?
too much	too many
a little	a few
more	more
enough	enough
a lot of	a lot of

There isn't **much** rain here in the summer.
Are there **many** hotels in the town?

How much money do you want?
How many states are there in the USA?

I've got **too much** work.
You've given me **too many** chips.

A little more cabbage, sir?
And **a few** more peas?

Could I have some **more** bread?
I'm afraid there are no **more** potatoes.

Have you got **enough** money? (~~. . . . money enough?~~)
There aren't **enough** buses from our village.

The children are making **a lot of** noise.
She's got **a lot of** problems.

We can also use these words and expressions without nouns.

How much does it cost?
'Do you like her?' 'Not **much**.'
I think about you **a lot**. (~~. . . . a lot of.~~)

We use *much* and *many* mostly in questions and negative sentences. In affirmative sentences, we more often use *a lot (of)*. Compare:

Have you got **many** friends?
I haven't got **many** friends.
She's got **a lot of** friends.

We use *too*, not *too much*, before an adjective/adverb when there is no noun. Compare:

Am I **too** early? (~~. . . too much early?~~)
You've got **too much** baggage.

Enough comes after an adverb, and after an adjective if there is no noun. Compare:

You're not driving **fast enough**.
Is the beer **cold enough** to drink?
We haven't got **enough cold** beer.

Other determiners

Both and *all*: position with verbs

- One-part verbs
  We **both read** *The Times*. (~~We read both . . . .~~)
  They **all went** home. (~~They went all home.~~)

- Two-part verbs
  We **have both got** bicycles. (~~We both have got . . . .~~)
  They **will all come**. (~~They all will come.~~)

- *Are/were*
  We **are both** tall. (~~We both are tall.~~)
  You **were all** wrong. (~~You all were wrong.~~)

Both/all/neither/one + *of* + pronoun

Both of them are very tall.
I wish I had time to talk to **all of you**.
Neither of us has got a cat.
One of us likes classical music, but the other doesn't.

Question words

Who

'**Who**'s that?' 'It's my brother.' (~~He's my brother.~~)
Who wrote *Gone with the Wind*? (~~Who did write . . . ?~~)
Who are you looking at? (~~Who you are . . . ?~~)

Which

'**Which** platform for the 3.49 train?' 'Platform 6.'
Which of you took my bike? (~~Who of you . . . ?~~)

What

'**What**'s your name?' 'Miriam Jackson.'
What does *coat* mean? (~~What means *coat*?~~)
What time does the next train leave?
  (*NOT usually* At what time . . . ?)
What sort of music do you like?
'**What** do you do?' 'I'm a student.' (~~I'm student.~~)
What a nice colour! (~~What nice colour!~~)

How

'My name's Ann Carter.' '**How** do you do?' '**How** do you do?'
'**How** are you?' 'Very well, thank you. And you?'
'**How** old are you?' 'I'm 35.'
How did the children travel back home?
  (~~How travelled the children . . . ?~~)

Where

'**Where**'s my pen?' 'Under your book.'
'**Where** are you from?' 'Egypt.'
Where was Brian born? (~~Where was born Brian?~~)

When

When did the Second World War start?
  (~~When started . . . ?~~)

Why

'**Why** did you come to Australia?' 'To learn English.'
  (~~For learn English.~~)

Question words as subject and object

When a question word is the subject of a sentence (or with the subject of a sentence), we make questions without *do*. Compare:

Who (*subject*) **wrote** the James Bond novels?
  (Who did write . . . ?)
Who (*object*) **do** you like in the class?

What (*subject*) **made** that noise? (What did make . . . ?)
What (*object*) **do** you want?

What animals (*subject*) **live** in trees? (. . . do live . . . ?)
What animals (*object*) **did** Hannibal take across the Alps? (What animals took Hannibal . . . ?)

How many children (*subject*) **came** to the party?
  (. . . did come . . . ?)
How many children (*object*) **did** you invite to the party?

Adjectives

Position of adjectives

Before nouns

Mary has got **green** eyes. (. . . greens eyes.)
Sheila has got **long dark** hair.

After *be*

John is quite **nice**.
My daughters are very **tall**. (. . . are very talls.)

Comparative and superlative adjectives

ONE-SYLLABLE ADJECTIVES

	Adjective	*Comparative*	*Superlative*
MOST ONE-SYLLABLE ADJECTIVES:	old	older	oldest
	short	shorter	shortest
	cheap	cheaper	cheapest
	young	younger (/'jʌŋgə(r)/)	youngest (/'jʌŋgɪst/)
	long	longer (/'lɒŋgə(r)/)	longest (/'lɒŋgɪst/)
ENDING IN -*e*:	late	later	latest
	fine	finer	finest
ENDING IN ONE VOWEL + ONE CONSONANT:	fat	fatter	fattest
	slim	slimmer	slimmest
	big	bigger	biggest
IRREGULAR:	good	better	best
	bad	worse	worst
	far	farther	farthest

TWO-SYLLABLE ADJECTIVES

	Adjective	*Comparative*	*Superlative*
ENDING IN -*y*:	happy	happier	happiest
	easy	easier	easiest
MOST OTHERS:	complete	**more** complete	**most** complete
	famous	**more** famous	**most** famous

LONGER ADJECTIVES

	Adjective	*Comparative*	*Superlative*
	interesting	**more** interesting	**most** interesting
	beautiful	**more** beautiful	**most** beautiful
	difficult	**more** difficult	**most** difficult

Using comparatives and superlatives

Comparatives

I'm **taller than** my mother.
She's **more intelligent** than me.

Superlatives

Who's **the oldest** person here?
I'm **the tallest** in my family.
It's **the most beautiful** place in the world.
  (. . . of the world.)
Which car is **the fastest**?
Which can carry **the most** people?

Modification of comparatives

She's **a bit older** than me.
A plane is **much faster** than a train.
A bus can carry **far more** people than a car.
A car costs **much less** than a plane.

Less and *least* with adjectives

Dürer looks **less happy than** the king.
My brother's **less self-confident than** me.
She's **the least selfish** person I know.

More and *most* with nouns

A plane has got **more wheels than** a pram.
A plane can carry **the most** people.

Less/least with uncountable nouns

I've got **less** free **time** than ever before in my life.
Who does **the least work** in this office?

Fewer/fewest with plural nouns

There are **fewer people** here than last week.
  (NOTE: . . . *less people* is also possible.)
The person who makes **the fewest mistakes** is not
  always the best.

Comparisons with *as*

(*Not*) *as* + adjective/adverb + *as*

I'm **as good-looking as** a film star.
He's not **as tall as** me.
Your car doesn't go **as fast as** ours.

(*Not*) *as much/many as*

She's got **as much** money **as** me.
A car hasn't got **as many** wheels **as** a lorry.
A bicycle doesn't cost **as much as** a motorbike.

As and *than*

faster **than** (faster as)
more beautiful **than**
as fast **as** (as fast than)

Note also:

the same **as**
different **from**

Adverbs

Adjectives and adverbs

We use adjectives before nouns and after *be*.
We use adverbs to give more information about verbs and adjectives.
Compare:

You've got a **nice face.** (*adjective*)
You **sing nicely.** (*adverb*)
  (You sing nice.)

I'm **angry** with you. (*adjective*)
She **spoke angrily.** (*adverb*)
  (She spoke angry.)

It's **terrible.** (*adjective*)
It's **terribly cold.** (*adverb*)
  (It's terrible cold.)

You speak **good English.** (*adjective*)
You **speak** English **well.** (*adverb*)
  (You speak English good.)

Spelling of *-ly* adverbs

		ADJECTIVE	ADVERB
MOST WORDS:		kind	kind**ly**
		careful	careful**ly** (carefuly)
		extreme	extreme**ly** (extremly)
ADJECTIVES ENDING IN -*y*:		happy	happ**ily**
		angry	angr**ily**
ADJECTIVES ENDING IN -*ble*:		comfortable	comforta**bly**

Position of adverbs

Don't put adverbs between the verb and the object.

She speaks English **well**. (~~She speaks well English.~~)
I opened the letter **carefully**. (~~I opened carefully the letter.~~)
I **never** read science fiction. (~~I read never science fiction.~~)

Frequency adverbs: how often?

How often?

How often do you go to the cinema?
Do you **ever** go to the opera?

From most to least often

I **always** have coffee for breakfast.
I **usually** have toast and butter.
I **very often** go away at weekends.
I **often** go out in the evenings.
I **sometimes** go to the cinema.
I don't stay at home **very often**.
I **occasionally** travel abroad.
I **hardly ever** eat fish.
I **never** play golf.

Position of frequency adverbs

– **One-part verbs**
  I **always have** coffee for breakfast.
      (~~I have always coffee . . .~~)
  I **very often go** away at weekends.
      (~~I go very often away . . .~~)

– **Two-part verbs**
  She **has always been** friendly to me.
      (~~She always has been . . .~~)
  We **were often invited** to her house.
      (~~We often were invited . . .~~)
  I **can never understand** what she says.
      (~~I never can understand . . .~~)

– *Am/are/is/was/were*
  She **is usually** late.
      (~~She usually is late.~~)
  I **am never** at home these days.
      (~~I never am at home . . .~~)

Regular frequency

I come here	every day.
	every three days.
	once a day.
	twice a week.
	three times a year.

Adverbs of degree

With adjectives

I'm	**not at all**	tired.
	not very	
	a bit	
	quite	
	very	
	extremely	

With verbs

I **very much** like football.
I **quite** like walking.
I don't **much** like washing up.
I don't like washing clothes **at all**.

Comparative and superlative adverbs

We usually make comparative and superlative adverbs with *more* and *most*.

Could you speak **more slowly**?
She sings **most beautifully**.

Exceptions: *faster, fastest; better, best.*
She can run **faster** than me.
I speak English **better** than my father.

Prepositions

Talking about time

I'll see you **at** ten o'clock.
        in the morning.
        on Thursday.
        on Thursday morning.
        on June 22nd.
        at the weekend.
I don't work **on** Saturdays.

I'll see you **in** three days.
   (= three days from now)

We go skiing every year **for** two weeks.
I've been here **for** six weeks.
           since Christmas.

I work **from** nine **to/until** six.
I'll be here **until** a quarter to three.

She only studies **before** exams.
I'm free **after** six o'clock.

half **past** nine
five **to** ten

No preposition

What time do you get up? (*NOT usually* At what time . . . ?)
I'll see you **this afternoon**.
I'll see you **next week**.
I saw her **last week**.

Talking about place

         on
⌐¬ ⌐¬ [in] ⌐¬
under   near

It's **on** the table. (~~. . . in the table.~~)
   under your chair.
   in the fridge.
   near the door.

in the living room
in a small flat
on the second floor
at No 53 Park Street
in Park Street
in London
in England

He **lived in** Saigon.
He **studied at** Saigon University.

I'm going **to** Edinburgh tomorrow. (~~. . . going at . . .~~)
I'll **arrive at** Waverley Station at 9.15.
   (~~. . . arrive to . . .~~)

She was the first woman to fly **across** the Atlantic.
                  round the world.

'Where are you **from**?' 'I'm **from** Ireland.'

He's **at** the disco.
   at the supermarket.
   at the doctor's.
   at the bus stop.
   at the station.
   at home. (~~at the home.~~)
   at work. (~~at the work.~~)
   at school. (~~at the school.~~)
   at lunch. (~~at the lunch.~~)
   in bed. (~~in the bed.~~)
   on his way to work.

It's **by** the reception desk.
   near the stairs.
   next to the post office.
   opposite the station.
   outside the window.
   behind the tree.
   in front of the tree.
   between those two trees.

Go straight on **for** 300 metres and it's **on** the right.

Our bedroom is **over** the living room.

He got **into** his car and drove away.
She got **out of** the car and went into the house.

No preposition

I want to go **home**. (~~. . . to home.~~)

Other uses of prepositions

Here's a letter **for** you.

the girl **in** jeans
the man **with** a beard
My sister looks **like** me.

We're all slim **except** Joe.

'How old is she?' '**Over** 20.'
             '**Under** 30.'

good **at** maths
good **at** running

the highest mountain **in** the world. (~~. . . of the world.~~)

We went to Spain **on** holiday.
We went there **by** bus/car/train/air.

I often think **about** you.
We were talking **about** money.

I can't go **without** sleep for very long.

Look at my new dress.
Would you like to **listen to** some music?
I'm **looking for** a sweater.

Putting things together

And; but; both . . . and; neither . . . nor

I went into the kitchen **and** looked in all the cupboards,
   but I couldn't find any sugar.
Both Ann **and** I like riding.
Neither Ann **nor** I can swim.

Because

She left university **because** she wanted to learn to fly.
Because you were so rude to me, I've decided not to see
   you again.

Conjunctions of time

When I'm bored I go and see friends.
I'll phone you **when** I get home.
   (. . . . when I will get home.)

As soon as the kettle boils, I'll make tea.
   (As soon as the kettle will boil . . . .)
Do you get up **as soon as** you wake up?

Before you buy something, do you always ask the price?
Always warm up **before** you go running.

After I leave school I'm going to travel.
   (After I will leave school . . . .)
Rest for a few minutes **after** you finish running.

Will you keep working **until** you're 60?

If

Ordinary tenses

If both parents have got blue eyes, their children will
   have blue eyes.
We usually go walking at the weekend **if** the weather's
   fine.
If you see a black cat, you'll have good luck.
   (If you will see . . . .)
I'll let you know **if** I hear from John.
   (. . . . if I will hear . . . .)

Unreal and improbable situations: past tense and *would*

If today **was** Sunday, I **would be** in bed.
If I **won** $1,000,000, I **would buy** a fast car.
   (If I would win . . . .)
He **would tell** us if he **knew**.
   (. . . . if he would know.)
It **would be** better if you **told** us the truth.

If I were etc.

We often use *were* instead of *was* after *if*, especially
in the expression *if I were you*.

If my French **was/were** better, I'd have a chance of
   passing the exams.
I wouldn't do that if I **were** you.

Talking about the past: past perfect and *would have* . . .

If his parents **had been** well off, he **would have gone** to
   university.
If he **hadn't worked** in the bank, he **wouldn't have gone**
   to Italy.
Where **would** he **have gone** if he **had decided** not to go
   to Italy?
If he **had joined** the army earlier he **would have been**
   sent to Germany.

If and *when*

If I get enough money, I'll travel round the world.
   (I may possibly get enough money.)
When I get older I'll stop playing rugby.
   (I will certainly get older.)

Reported speech

Reported statements and thoughts

'You **will** never get married.'
Maria **said** (that) I **would** never get married.
   (Maria said that I will . . .)

'We're going to take ten litres of water.'
They **said** (that) they **were** going to take . . .

'I **like** my boss.'
She **said** (that) she **liked** her boss.
   (She said that she likes her boss.)

I **didn't** realise that you **liked** your boss.
I **thought** you **hated** him.

'I've been to Venice.'
He **told** Janet that he **had** been to Venice.

Say and tell

Fred **said** that he lived in Paris and California.
   (Fred said Janet that . . .)
He **told Janet** that he had been photographing
   the President. (He told that . . .)

Reported questions

'Where **do** you **work?**'
She asked me where I **worked.**
   (She asked me where I work.)
   (She asked me where did I work.)
   (She asked me 'where did I work'.)
   (She asked me where did I work?)

'Where **is** your home?'
She **asked** me where my home **was.**
   (She asked me where was my home.)

'Do you like living there?'
She asked me **if** I liked living there.

Reported instructions and requests

'You must tidy up afterwards.'
She **told** him **to tidy** up afterwards.

'Please don't make so much noise.'
She **asked** him **not to make** so much noise.

Relative clauses

Who, that and where

Paula is a young doctor **who plays tennis.**
Lewis is a company director **who eats too much.**
A watch is a thing **that tells you the time.**
A hat is a thing **that you wear on your head.**
A platform is a place **where you wait for a train.**

Leaving out object pronouns

A hat is a thing (that) you wear on your head.
I often give presents to people (who) I like.

Joining sentences

Structuring paragraphs

When I . . . , I usually . . . **First of all,** I . . . **Then** I . . . **and**
. . . **Next** I . . . **After that** I . . . **Then** I . . . **until** . . .
Before I . . . , I . . . **Finally** I . . .

Linking expressions

Look . . .
You're **just** too old.
Well, yes, OK.
So what?
You haven't **even** got any money.

Well, yes, I know.
What's he like, **then?**
Well, you know.
No, **actually,** he isn't.
perhaps/maybe

perhaps/maybe not
I don't know.
on the other hand
I do think my eyes are too small, **though.**
Still, they're pretty.

Position of prepositions and adverb particles

Prepositions in questions

Where are you **from?** (From where are you?)
What are you looking **at?**
Who are you talking **about?**

Prepositions in relative clauses

A chair is a thing (that) you sit **on.**
A tap is a thing (that) water comes out **of.**

Adjective + infinitive + preposition

She's **easy** to work **with.**
He's **nice to talk to.**

Position of adverb particle

Could you **pick that book up?**
   OR: Could you **pick up that book?**
Could you **pick it up?** (Could you pick up it?)

You'd better **take your sweater off.**
   OR: You'd better **take off your sweater.**
You'd better **take it off.** (You'd better take off it.)

Problems with some words

Verbs with two objects

Some verbs (for example *bring, give, lend, show, tell*) often have
two objects.

Could you bring **me some water**?
Can I give **you a little more coffee**?
Could you lend **me some sugar**?

Could you show **me some black sweaters**, please?
I told **the policemen my address**.

Lend and *borrow*

Lend is like *give*; *borrow* is like *take*.

Could you **lend** me some sugar?
Could I **borrow** some sugar (from you)?
   (~~Could I borrow you some sugar?~~)

Like and *would like*

Like means 'enjoy'; *would like* means 'want'.

'**Do** you **like** dancing?'   'Yes, I do. I go dancing
   every weekend.'
'**Would** you **like** to dance?'   'No, thanks. I'm tired.'

Like + object + infinitive

Would you **like me to switch** the lights on?

Get

1. *Get* + object = 'obtain', 'receive', 'fetch'.

   Where can I **get some stamps**?
   I **get a letter** from my mother every week.
   Can you **get me some bread**, please?

2. *Get* + adjective = 'become'.

   It's **getting late**.
   If you work too hard you'll **get tired**.

3. *Get* + adverb particle/preposition = 'move'.

   What time do you usually **get up**?
   It takes me an hour to **get to** work.
   Get on the bus outside the station, and **get off**
      at Park Street.
   Get out!!

4. *Have got* = 'have', 'possess', 'be related to'.

   You've **got** beautiful eyes.
   Have you **got** any brothers or sisters?

5. *Get lost, married, killed* = 'become lost, married
   etc.'

   We went for a walk and **got lost** in the woods.
   She's **getting married** next week.
   He **got killed** in a car crash.

Be like, *look like* and *look*

'What **is** she **like**?' ('~~How is she?~~')
   'She's a bit shy, but very nice.'

He **looks like** a footballer.
I think he **looks more like** a businessman.
She **looks like** her mother.

She **looks** bad-tempered.
You **look** tired.

Born

I **was born** in 1936. (~~I am born . . .~~)
When **were** you **born**?

Agree

I agree. (~~I am agree.~~)
He doesn't agree.

Still, yet and already

We use *still* to talk about *continuation*.

John's **still** in bed.

We use *yet* to ask whether *expected actions* have happened, or to say that they haven't.

Has John got up **yet**?
He hasn't got up **yet**.

We use *already* to say things have happened *earlier than expected*.

Susan is **already** dressed.

Such and so

We use *such* before nouns (with or without adjectives).

She's **such a good dancer**.
He's **such a handsome man**.
They're **such fools**.

We use *so* before adjectives (without nouns).

She's **so good**.
He's **so handsome**.
They're **so stupid**.

Conversational grammar

Leaving out subjects

'What did you do?' '(I) had lunch with her.'
(It) sounds like a boring day.
'Did anything interesting happen?' '(I) don't think so. (I) can't remember.'

Auxiliary verbs without main verbs

Short answers

'Is it raining?' 'Yes, it **is**.'
'**Have** you got a cold?' 'No, I **haven't**.'
'**Can** you speak French?' 'Yes, I **can** a bit.'
'**Are** you ready?' 'No, I'm **not**.'
'**Do** you like skiing?' 'Yes, I **do**.'
'**Did** you sleep well?' 'No, I **didn't**.'
'Give my love to Andy.' 'I **will**.'

Showing interest: reply questions

'It's raining.' '**Is** it?'
'I've got a cold.' 'Oh, **have** you?'
'My father **can** speak five languages.' '**Can** he?'
'I'm Pisces.' '**Are** you?'
'I love skiing.' '**Do** you really?'
'I **slept** badly last night.' 'Oh, **did** you?'

So am I etc.

'I've got a pink Rolls-Royce.' '**So have I**.' 'I **haven't**.'
'I'm tired.' '**So am I**.' 'I'm **not**.'
'Mary **can** swim.' '**So can Alice**.' 'Louise **can't**.'
'I **go** skiing twice a year.' '**So do I**.' 'I **don't**.'
'John **phoned** last night.' '**So did your mother**.'

Question tags

| It is . . . , isn't it?
You **will** . . . , won't you?
She **can** . . . , can't she?
They **have** . . . , haven't they?
You **remember** . . . , don't you?
She **likes** . . . , doesn't she?

It **isn't** . . . , is it?
You **won't** . . . , will you?
She **can't** . . . , can she?
They **haven't** . . . , have they?
You **don't** . . . , do you? |

It's raining, **isn't it**?
You'll tell Ann, **won't you**?
She likes fish, **doesn't she**?
Joe can't swim, **can he**?
The children haven't come back yet, **have they**?
You didn't see Lucy on your way, **did you**?

Intonation of question tags

Real questions

'You're French, aren't you?' 'No, I'm Swiss.'

Asking for agreement

'Nice day, isn't it?' 'Yes, lovely.'

Doing things in English

Meeting and greeting

Introductions; meeting people

'Joe, this is Pat.' 'How do you do?'
  'How do you do?'
I'd like to introduce . . .
This is . . .
Do you know . . . ?
May I introduce myself? My name's . . .
Excuse me, aren't you . . . ?
I'm glad to meet you.
I'm sorry. I didn't catch your name.
Nice to see you again.
Where are you from?
Whereabouts in . . . ?

Formal greetings

Good morning/afternoon/evening.
Goodbye / Good night.

Informal greetings

Hi/Hello.
Bye / Goodbye / See you.

Asking about health

'How are you?' 'Very well, thanks.'
  'Fine, thanks. And you?'
  'Not too bad.'

Asking for personal information

'Where are you from?' 'Scotland.'
'Where do you live?' 'In Edinburgh.'
'Where do you work?' 'In a small shop in George
  Street.'
'What's your phone number?' '7623305.' (Seven six
  two, double three oh five.)

'What newspaper do you read?' *The Independent.*
'How do you travel to work?' 'By bus.'
'What sort of books do you like?' 'Science fiction.'
'Are you interested in politics?' 'Yes, I am.'

Opinions, likes and dislikes

'**How do you like** this place?' '**Great / Not bad / Not
  much / Terrible.**'
Do you like modern jazz?
What do you think of the government?
What's your **favourite** food?
I like dancing **very much**.

I **quite** like sport.
It's **OK**.
I like football **best**.
I **hate** shopping.
I **don't** like classical music **at all**.
'Do you like travelling?' '**It depends.**'

Apologising

'**Excuse me**, is your name Fred Andrews?'
'No, **I'm sorry**, it's not. It's Jake Barker.'
'**Pardon?**'

'It's Jake Barker.'
'Oh, **I'm sorry.**'
'**That's all right.**'

Inviting and answering invitations

'Are you doing anything this evening? **Would you like**
  to see a film?'
'**I don't know**, I'm a bit tired. **I don't really want** to go
  out tonight.'
'Well, **what about** tomorrow?'
'**Let me look in my diary. No, I'd love to**, but **I'm afraid**
  I'm not free. I'm going to a concert in London.'
'**How about** Thursday?'

'Thursday's **a bit difficult. Let's** do something at the
  weekend. Are you free?'
'**Perhaps.** Yes, **why not?**'
'**How about** Saturday? **Shall we** have dinner?'
'**What a** nice idea!'
'OK. **See you** about eight o'clock.'
'**Could it be earlier?** Half past seven?'
'Right, see you then.'

Making suggestions

'I haven't got anything to wear.' '**What/How about**
  your blue dress?'
Why don't you borrow something of mine?

Why not borrow something of mine?
I'll lend you my new shoes.
'**Shall I** iron it for you?' 'If you really don't mind.'

Discussion: opinions and advice

I think we **should** take a lot of water.
You **shouldn't** mend it with the wheels on.
Why don't you turn it sideways?
Don't forget to put it on the table.
Remember to take the wheels off first.
It would be better to turn it upside down.

That's right.
You're right.
I think you're wrong.
I agree. (~~I am agree.~~)
I don't agree.

Asking for and giving permission

Do you mind if I | sit here?
| open the window?
| smoke?
| look at your paper?

I'm sorry, it's not free.
Well, it's a bit cold.
Well, I'd rather you didn't.
Well, I'm reading it myself, actually.

Not at all.
No, please do.
Go ahead.

Asking for things; asking for help; borrowing and lending

Can you give me a hand? (*informal*)
Could you (possibly) help me for a few minutes?
  (*more formal*)

Can you lend me a stamp?
I'm sorry to trouble you, but could you lend me
  some sugar?
Could you possibly lend me your car?
Could I borrow your keys **for a moment**?

Yes, **here you are.**
Yes, **of course.**

I'm sorry, **I need it/them.**
I'm afraid I haven't got one/any.
I'm sorry, **I'm afraid** I can't.

Offers and replies

Shall I open it for you?
No thanks. I can do it myself.

I'll answer it, **shall I?**
That's very kind of you.

Can I hang your coat up for you?
No thanks. I'll keep it on.

Would you like some toast?
I'd love some.

Would you like some tea?
I'd prefer coffee, if you've got some.

Would you like to dance?
I'd love to.

Would you like to go and see a film this evening?
Not this evening, thanks. Perhaps another time?

Would you like me to carry that for you?
Thank you very much.

Telling people to do things

Please hurry!
Take your time.
Don't worry.
Look.
Come in.

Wait here, please.
Be careful.
Follow me, please.
Look out!

Restaurants: ordering and asking

I'll start with soup, please, and then **I'll have** roast beef.
Chicken **for me**, please.
Could you bring me a beer?
Just some water, please.

a little more coffee
Could you bring us **the bill**, please?
Is service **included**?

Shopping

'Can I help you?' 'I'm just looking.'
'I'm looking for a sweater.' 'Here's a lovely one.'
What a lovely sweater! (~~What lovely sweater!~~)
What nice shoes!
Those aren't very nice. I don't like that very much.
Can I look round?
Can I try them on?
'Have you got anything in black?' 'I'll just see.'

'No, I'm afraid I haven't. Would you like to try these?'
  (~~Would you like try these?~~)
How much are they? How much is it?
I'll take them, please.
I'd like a red one.
I'd like to look at some watches.
  (~~I'd like look at some watches.~~)

Asking for things when you don't know the words

a thing **with** a hole / **with** a handle

a machine **for making** holes
a tool **for cutting** wood
a thing **for putting** pieces of paper together

some material **for making** curtains
some liquid **for cleaning** windows
some powder **for washing** clothes
some stuff **for killing** insects

Asking for and giving directions

Excuse me. Where's the nearest post office, please?
Excuse me. Is there a post office near here, please?

It's over there by the police station.
First on the right, then second on the left.
Take the first right, second left, then straight on.

How far is it?

About a hundred metres.
About a hundred yards.

Thank you very much.
Not at all.

I'm sorry. I don't know.
Thank you anyway.

Talking about feeling ill

I feel ill.
What's the matter?
My eyes hurt.   My arm hurts.
Do they hurt / Does it hurt very badly?

I've got a (bad) cold / a (bad) headache /
   (bad) toothache / flu / a temperature.
   (*American*: a toothache; the flu)
Why don't you see the doctor / dentist?

Telephoning

Can/Could I speak to . . . ?
This is . . .
Is that . . . ? (*American*: Is this . . . ?)

He/She's not in.
Can I take a message?

Describing

a woman **with** dark hair
a woman **who has** dark hair
a **dark-haired** woman

a person **with** a thin face
a person **who has** a thin face
a **thin-faced** person

Probability and certainty

I know	she's at home.
I'm sure	
I think	
Perhaps	

She's	**certainly**	at home.
	probably	

She	**must**	be at home.
	may	
	might	
	could	
	can't	

Talking about ages, heights and weights

The Great Pyramid **is** 4,500 years **old**.
It **is** 135 metres **high**.
The car **is** 4 metres **long**.
The statue **weighs** three kilos.

Lucy **is** four months **old**.
Her mother **is** 40 (years old).
I **am** 1 metre 91.
I **weigh** 85 kilos.

She's **over** 21 and **under** 30.

How old/tall are you?
How much do you weigh?

Formal and informal language

MORE FORMAL	LESS FORMAL
Hello.	Hi.
How are you?	How's it going?
Very well, thank you.	Not too bad.
Goodbye.	See you.
Excuse me.	Hey!
Could you lend me . . . ?	Have you got . . . ?
Thank you very much.	Thanks a lot.
Do you mind if . . . ?	Is it OK if . . . ?

Asking about English

What's this? What's this called in English, please?
What are these?
Is this a pen or a pencil? Is this a lighter?
How do you say *arroyo* in English?
What's the English for *arroyo*?
What does *shy* mean? (~~What means *shy*?~~)
What do you say when . . . ?

Can you explain this word/expression/sentence?
How do you pronounce k–n–e–w?
How do you spell that word?
Is this correct: . . . ?
I don't understand this.
Could you speak more slowly, please?

Dates

WRITE	SAY
14 Jan(uary) 1990 14.1.90 (GB) 1.14.90 (US)	January the fourteenth, nineteen ninety (GB) January fourteenth . . . (US)
5 Apr(il) 1892	April the fifth, eighteen ninety-two
9 Dec(ember) 1600	December the ninth, sixteen hundred
14 May 1906	May the fourteenth, nineteen hundred and six OR: . . . nineteen oh six

---

Writing formal letters

> Flat 6
> Monument House
> Castle Street
> Newcastle NE1 2HH
>
> 12 September 1990
>
> Dear Mr Bell,
>
> I am arriving at Waverley Station, Edinburgh . . .
>
> . . .
>
> I look forward to seeing you.
>
> Yours sincerely,
>
> Paul Sanders

Additional reading

Chant

This poem comes from the Dinka people of the Sudan.

In the time when Dendid created[1] all things,
He created the sun,
And the sun is born, and dies, and comes again;
He created the moon,
And the moon is born, and dies, and comes again;
He created the stars,
And the stars are born, and die, and come again;
He created man,
And man is born, and dies, and never comes again.

(from *Voices from Twentieth-Century Africa*)

created[1]: made something new

A person who happens to be blind[1]

John Bailey is blind and has a guide dog named Elgar. John finds that many people don't know what to do or say when they meet someone like him who can't see. Here he explains how to behave towards blind people and their dogs.

- Remember I am an ordinary person, just blind. You don't need to shout or talk to me as if I cannot understand. If you are giving me a cup of tea or coffee, then I can tell you how I take it – you don't have to ask my wife.
- I can walk more easily with you than by myself, but please don't grab my arm; let me take yours. When I am with Elgar, I will drop the handle on his harness to tell him he is no longer working, and I will take your left arm with my right. I will keep half a step behind so that I can feel it when we are about to go up or down steps or a kerb. Going downstairs, I prefer to hold the handrail if there is one.
- It is always nice for me to know who is in the room with us, so please do introduce me – and to the cat and dog! And if you come into a room where I am, please do speak so I know you're there.
- If I am somewhere new, you will have to guide me to a chair and tell me about things in my way or on the floor. Don't forget about lampshades – they often stick out into my path and I do hate breaking things!
- At mealtimes, I may ask for a little help, particularly with cutting up meat. And you can make my meal a lot more enjoyable by telling me where which food is on my plate – for example 'Chicken at 9 o'clock, peas at 3 o'clock and potatoes at 6 o'clock – and a glass of water at 2 o'clock.'
- Words like 'see' don't worry me, so you needn't be embarrassed about using them; I use them too. I am always glad to see people.
- Elgar loves attention, but remember never to distract[2] him when he's working, as my safety depends on him. And, of course, please don't feed[3] him titbits – he gets very properly fed at home and will get fat if you feed him too!
- The most important thing of all is not to think of me as a blind person; I am a person who happens to be blind.

(from *Forward* – the Journal of The Guide Dogs for the Blind Association)

happens to be blind[1]: is blind by chance
distract[2]: make him interested in something else
feed[3]: give food to

Decide if the following are true (*T*) or false (*F*).

1. John likes people to help him walk.
2. He doesn't worry if he breaks things.
3. He has dinner at 9 o'clock.
4. He is blind but he can see people a little bit.
5. He doesn't like people to give his dog food.

There doesn't seem any need to be married

At the age of 40, ballet dancer Lesley Collier has just become the mother of twin boys. She has been married twice and now lives with the twins' father, Guy Niblett, who is also a ballet dancer.

Lesley has lived with Guy for just over three years, six months longer than she has been divorced from her second husband, ballet critic Nicholas Dromgoole. Nicholas was 19 years her senior. Guy is 11 years her junior, blond and deliciously handsome with twinkling blue eyes.

'I have never managed to find someone of my own age,' she smiled. 'The relationship with Guy was something I didn't want to get into, because he is so much younger. I worried terribly about it. But when I bought my flat [after she left her second husband] he began to stay nights and I kept saying "I must not make this permanent[1]." Then he moved in and I still said "I must not make it permanent," but now I feel it's important for us to be together and I've stopped worrying.

'Certainly when I was the younger partner in a relationship with Nicholas the age difference didn't worry me, although he worried about it. I think it bothers the older person rather than the younger one. Nicholas gave our relationship ten years.[2] He knew I would go off and find a younger man. But we have remained good friends and he loves the twins.' Will she marry again?

'I doubt it. We have a very happy relationship. There doesn't seem any need to be married and I actually don't want to.'

(from an article in *The Mail on Sunday YOU Magazine*)

permanent[1]: lasting forever
gave our relationship ten years[2]: thought our relationship would last about ten years

Look carefully at the text to decide if the following are true (*T*) or false (*F*).

1. Nicholas is 59 now.
2. Guy is 29 now.
3. 'her senior' means 'younger than her'.
4. Lesley has been divorced for 3½ years.
5. Guy was 29 when he and Lesley started living together.

What do you dream about?

Most of us dream for about two hours each night and almost always about people: for 45 per cent of the time about people we know and 55 per cent those that we do not. Men are twice as likely to dream of men as of women and for both sexes only 30 per cent of dreams are of groups of people, compared with 70 per cent about individual characters.

Apparently we rarely dream about people in the public eye but some 20 per cent of our dreams include our family. Mothers appear 34 per cent of the time, fathers 27 per cent, brothers 14 per cent and sisters 12 per cent. On the whole, the themes of our dreams tend towards the unhappy, with fear occurring in 40 per cent, anger in 18 per cent and sadness in 6 per cent.

(from *Vital Statistics* by Gyles Brandreth)

Were you surprised by the facts in the passage? Write what things *you* dream about.

Section C

Women, transport and safety

Read this with a dictionary – but don't look up more than eight of the underlined words.

Many women are attacked when using transport or driving. What can they do to avoid this?

Police advice when:

Driving
- Get your car serviced and check petrol regularly.
- Make the effort to join a breakdown organisation.
- Keep a map handy.
- Make sure you have change for emergency calls.
- Park in well-lit, preferably busy areas. On returning, have your key ready. Check the back seat. Keep windows closed and doors locked.
- If you think you're about to break down on a motorway, park as near to an emergency phone as you can.
- If you think you're being followed, drive until you reach a busy place or a police station.

Using a mini-cab[1]
- Never get in a cab you haven't ordered.
- Use a cab firm you know, ask what colour and kind of car is likely to come, try to get the driver's name.

Using tubes, trains or buses
- Sit near women or the driver when on buses.
- On tubes and trains try to sit in the compartment nearest the guard or driver. Never sit in a single compartment or an empty one. Move if you have to.
- At the station, wait near the ticket office.

Other action
- If you work late, ask for a cab home to be paid for you.
- When out with friends, try to see each other home as far as possible. Ring and check they've all arrived.

(adapted from an article in *Company* magazine)

mini-cab[1]: a kind of taxi

Talk

This story, about a day when everything began to talk, is told by the Ashanti people of Ghana.

Once, not far from the city of Accra on the Gulf of Guinea, a country man went out to his garden to dig up[1] some yams to take to market. While he was digging, one of the yams said to him: 'Well, at last you're here. You never weeded[2] me, but now you come around with your digging stick. Go away and leave me alone!'

The farmer turned around and looked at his cow in surprise.

'Did you say something?' he asked.

The cow said nothing, but the man's dog spoke up.

'It wasn't the cow who spoke to you,' the dog said. 'It was the yam. The yam says leave him alone.'

The man became angry, so he took his knife and cut a branch from a palm tree to hit his dog. Just then the palm tree said: 'Put that branch down!'

The man was getting very upset and he started to throw the palm branch away, but the palm branch said: 'Man, put me down softly!'

He put the branch down gently on a stone, and the stone said: 'Hey, take that thing off me.'

This was enough, and the frightened farmer started to run for his village. On the way he met a fisherman with a fish trap on his head.

'What's the hurry?' the fisherman asked.

'My yam said, "Leave me alone!" Then the dog said, "Listen to what the yam says!" When I went to whip the dog with a palm branch the tree said, "Put that branch down!" Then the palm branch said, "Do it softly!" Then the stone said, "Take that thing off me!"'

'Is that all?' the man with the fish trap asked. 'Is that so frightening?'

'Well,' the man's fish trap said, 'did he take it off the stone?'

'Wah!' the fisherman shouted. He began to run with the farmer, and on the trail they met a weaver with a bundle of cloth on his head.

'Where are you going in such a rush?' he asked them.

'My yam said, "Leave me alone!"' the farmer said. 'The dog said, "Listen to what the yam says!" The tree said, "Put that branch down!" The branch said, "Do it softly." And the stone said, "Take that thing off me!"'

'And then,' the fisherman continued, 'the fish trap said, "Did he take it off?"'

'That's nothing to get excited about,' the weaver said, 'no reason at all.'

'Oh yes it is,' his bundle of cloth said. 'If it happened to you, you'd run too!'

'Wah!' the weaver shouted. He started running with the other men. They ran to the house of the chief. The chief's servants brought his stool out, and he came and sat on it to listen to their complaints.

'I went out to my garden to dig yams,' the farmer said. 'Then everything began to talk! My yam said, "Leave me alone!" My dog said, "Pay attention to your yam!" The tree said, "Put that branch down!" The branch said, "Do it softly!" And the stone said, "Take it off me!"'

'And my fish trap said, "Well, did he take if off?"' the fisherman said.

'And my cloth said, "You'd run too!"' the weaver said.

The chief listened to them patiently, but he couldn't stop himself from getting angry.

'Now this really is a wild story,' he said at last. 'You'd better all go back to your work before I punish you for disturbing the peace[3].'

So the men went away and the chief shook his head and mumbled to himself, 'Stupid stories like that upset the community.'

'Fantastic, isn't it?' his stool said. 'Imagine a talking yam!'

(adapted from *Voices from Twentieth-Century Africa*)

dig up[1]: take plants out of the ground using a stick
weeded[2]: took away unwanted plants
disturbing the peace[3]: making people angry or frightened

Match the words and phrases from the text (*1–6*) with their meanings (*A–F*). Example: *1E*.

1. upset the community
2. cloth
3. yam
4. punish
5. weaver
6. stool

A. a kind of vegetable
B. a small chair with no back and three legs
C. someone who makes cloth
D. something you can make clothes with
E. make people angry or frightened
F. do something unpleasant to a person who has done wrong (e.g. send them to prison)

Section D

I'll never forget . . .

Twenty-six-year-old barrister Annette Henry will never forget the romantic evening that ended with a splash[1] . . .

'I was on holiday in Cyprus with my parents and I'd met this nice boy, Pambos. One evening – wanting to give me a special surprise – he took me to this lovely restaurant with tables round a swimming pool. We were gazing into each other's eyes in the moonlight when to my surprise I saw Mum and Dad walk in – they'd picked the same restaurant! I was just about to go over when Dad pulled out a chair for himself, started sitting down . . . and then suddenly he was gone! He hadn't realised in the darkness that the swimming pool was just behind him. "I thought it was a dance floor," he said moments later when he came up. Luckily he was OK, but my romantic evening was dampened[2] too . . .'

(adapted from a letter to *Best* magazine)

splash[1]: what happens when something hits water hard
dampened[2]: 1) made something a little wet
2) made something less exciting

Choose the best summary.

A. Annette was with a new boyfriend in a restaurant. Her parents came in and her father fell in the swimming pool, which he thought was a dance floor. After that the romance of the evening was gone.

B. Annette's new boyfriend wanted to give her a surprise and invited her parents to the same restaurant. Her father fell in the swimming pool, which was a surprise for everyone. After that the romance of the evening was gone.

A mirror, an echo

Ved Mehta became blind at the age of three after a serious illness. Although he couldn't see, he tried to do everything that normal children did. His father also wanted Ved to live as normal a life as possible, and he later sent him to a school for blind and partially sighted children. Here Ved describes how he came to understand the idea of a mirror.

Whenever I asked Paran, from the boy's side of the classroom, "What are you doing, Paran?" she would say, "I'm looking into my mirror."

"What do you see in a mirror?"

"My reflection."

"What is that?"

"It's my double."

"But how can it be your double? The mirror is thin and flat."

"You have to be able to see to understand."

I could not work out the puzzle of Paran and the mirror until some time after Abdul and I stumbled onto[1] a heavy stone slab in the cellar. We moved it and discovered that under it was a big, sloping hole. We got down into the hole. I was frightened and wanted to run back, because the tunnel – for that was what it seemed to be – was knee-deep in water, and I could hear things splashing[2] and swimming, scuttling and buzzing. The little noises were picked up and repeated all around me, until it seemed that the whole tunnel was full of ghosts[3], snakes and wasps.

"I'm getting out of here!" I shouted.

"I'm getting out of here!" they shouted back.

Abdul and I almost fell over each other getting out of the tunnel.

We put the stone back over the hole and didn't go near it for a few days. But one day I told Deoji about the tunnel.

"That's an old, unused sewer," he said. "I don't know what things were swimming down there. But the sound you heard was an echo."

"What is an echo?"

"It's when your voice bounces back from the walls and the ceiling."

"Why doesn't it do that everywhere?"

"You have to be in a tight corner or the voice will escape."

After that, I would often go down to the slab of stone, move it a chink[4], and shout, "Hello, there!" As I listened to the echo, I felt that, like Paran, I was looking into a mirror.

(from *Vedi* by Ved Mehta)

stumbled onto[1]: found by chance
splashing[2]: hitting the water noisily
ghosts[3]: spirits of dead people
move it a chink[4]: move it to make a small opening

To Ved the idea of an echo is similar to the idea of a mirror. He found his echo 'down there' in a hole. Draw lines to the left for words that mean something like *echo* or *mirror*, to the right for words that mean something like *hole*.

echo/mirror   *hole*

           reflection
           double
           cellar
           tunnel
           shout back
           sewer ————
           bounce back

Section E

Singing in the plane

A 55-year-old British pilot sang throughout the night to keep from falling asleep and freezing to death after his plane crashed into a snow-covered forest in Labrador.

Mr William Loverseed, of Wellington Gardens, Selsey, near Chichester, kept singing "All I Want is a Room Somewhere," over and over.

"It was the most appropriate[1] song I could think of," he said.

Mr Loverseed was ferrying a single-engined Piper Cherokee from the United States to Britain for his employers, South Coast Aviation of Chichester. He ran into unexpected freezing rain which built up ice quickly on the wings and fuselage, forcing the aircraft down.

He said: "I sat there wrestling with the controls[2] until I hit something in the dark, and it was trees."

His right ankle was broken by the impact and, unable to walk to safety, he squeezed into a warmer suit.

"My main occupation the whole night was to keep awake so I would not freeze," he said.

Sixteen hours later a Canadian armed forces helicopter heard signals from his emergency transmitter and picked him up.

(from the *Daily Telegraph*)

most appropriate[1]: best for that situation
controls[2]: things you use to make a machine stop, turn etc.

Match the words and phrases from the text (*1–7*) with their meanings (*A–G*). Example *1C*.

1. throughout	A. water at 0°C
2. keep from	B. again and again
3. freezing to death	C. for all of
4. over and over	D. crash
5. ferrying	E. avoid
6. ice	F. dying of cold
7. impact	G. taking

Snake!

When he was a young man the writer Roald Dahl went to work in Tanzania (then called Tanganyika). There he saw a fight to the death between Salimu, an African servant, and a deadly snake.

One morning I was shaving myself in the bathroom of our Dar es Salaam house, and gazing out of the window into the garden. I was watching Salimu as he slowly raked[1] the gravel[2] on the front drive. Then I saw the snake. It was six feet long and thick as my arm and quite black. It was a mamba, and there was no doubt that it had seen Salimu and was gliding fast over the gravel straight towards him.

I flung myself toward the open window and yelled in Swahili, "Salimu! Salimu! Beware huge snake! Behind you! Quickly quickly!"

There was not much Salimu could do. He knew it was useless to run because a mamba at full speed could travel as fast as a galloping horse. It would reach him in another five seconds. I leant out of the window and held my breath. Salimu swung round and faced the snake. He crouched very low with one leg behind the other like a runner about to start a hundred yard sprint[3], and he was holding the long rake out in front of him. He raised it, but no higher than his shoulder, and he stood there for those long four or five seconds absolutely motionless[4], watching the great black deadly snake as it glided so quickly over the gravel towards him.

He waited until the very last moment when the mamba was not more than five feet away and then *wham!* Salimu struck first. He brought the metal prongs of the rake down hard right on to the middle of the mamba's back and he held the rake there with all his weight, leaning forward now and jumping up and down to put more weight on the fork in an effort to pin the snake to the ground. I saw the blood spurt where the prongs had gone right into the snake's body and then I rushed downstairs. Outside on the drive Salimu was still there pressing with both hands on the rake and the great snake was writhing and twisting[5] and throwing itself about, and I shouted to Salimu in Swahili, "What shall I do?"

"It is all right now, bwana!" he shouted back. "I have broken its back and it cannot travel forward any more! Stand away, bwana! Stand well away and leave it to me!"

Salimu lifted the rake and jumped away and the snake went on writhing and twisting but it was quite unable to travel in any direction. The boy went forward and hit it accurately and very hard on the head with the metal end of the rake and suddenly the snake stopped moving. Salimu let out a great sigh[6] and passed a hand over his forehead. Then he looked at me and smiled.

"Asanti, bwana," he said, "asanti sana," which simply means, "Thank you, bwana. Thank you very much."

(from *Going Solo* by Roald Dahl)

raked[1]: A rake is a tool with a long handle and metal teeth like a comb. The teeth are called 'prongs'. To rake is to make things flat and smooth with a rake.
gravel[2]: small stones
sprint[3]: a short fast race
absolutely motionless[4]: without moving at all
writhing and twisting[5]: turning its body
sigh[6]: the sound you make when you are sad, tired etc., by breathing out loudly

Put these sentences into the right order.

a. Salimu hit the snake on the back with his rake.
b. Salimu smiled at Roald Dahl and thanked him.
c. Roald Dahl ran to help Salimu.
d. The snake saw Salimu and started moving towards him.
e. Roald Dahl was shaving and watching Salimu at work.
f. Salimu hit the snake on the head.
g. Roald Dahl saw the snake and shouted to Salimu.

Queens of chess

Read this with a dictionary – but don't look up more than one or two words in any paragraph.

She's just turned 12, goes to a table tennis club every morning, likes pop music and is good, but not outstanding, at lessons.

An ordinary girl, she would have no particular claim on history except that she plays chess better, by at least a year, than anyone of her age ever has done – including Kasparov, Fischer and Short.

In an age which sometimes seems to produce chess prodigies off the assembly line, Judit Polgar of Hungary and her sisters, Zsofia and Zsuzsa, are changing people's ideas about women chess players.

Judit qualified this year, at 11, for the international master's norm (one step below a grand master) at men's level, a performance which the Kasparovs and Shorts of this world did not achieve until they were 14 or 15. Zsofia, aged 13, is a phenomenon in her own right, having qualified as a grand master (female rank) and also beaten male grand masters.

But they may be remembered most for changing a very old idea – that there are some things that women can never do as well as men.

Klara, their mother, said that when she and her husband, Laszlo, a psychology lecturer, decided to encourage their children to do something well through early specialisation they hadn't thought of chess. That happened when their first child, Zsuzsa, was aged four and discovered some horse-like figures in a box. She dropped her other special interest, mathematics, and hasn't looked back since.

Laszlo has successfully tested his theory that women have been less good than men at chess only because of discrimination through social attitudes and lack of proper facilities and training. The success of the Polgar sisters, helped by a few other girl prodigies, has already dealt with one of the two remaining questions of chess – why women traditionally have been much less good than men. The other is whether computers will ever be able consistently to beat grand masters. They haven't yet, but they are learning fast.

(adapted from an article in the *Guardian* by Victor Keegan)

Rich man, poor man

Harold Albert, the richest man in the world, lives in the small town of Bird in Kansas, USA. At the age of 14 he began working in his parents' store. There he met his wife, Louie.

HAROLD: When we got married, my folks said we could have the running of the store with my sister. So we got married in the church in the morning, then after we'd had something to eat everyone together, then her and me and my sister, we went back to the store and we opened it up and it was business as usual for the rest of the day. And that's how it was, from that day onwards all we did was work.

The only time we shut the store the whole year round was two hours at noon on Christmas Day, so we could eat our Christmas dinner. And people used to come by Christmas afternoon, they'd say "Where were you? I thought something was wrong. I was by an hour ago for some butter and the store was closed."
LOUIE: Hard work but we loved it.
HAROLD: Every minute.

(Then an oil company came looking for oil[1].)

LOUIE: When the oil came into our lives, that was when all the headaches came too.
HAROLD: One day they [the oil company] found they had a hole that had some oil. We had some little piece of land we owned ourselves out that way, and they said they'd do a test drill there too. And that one, the one on our land, before we knew what was happening, it was making not ten barrels a day but fifty barrels a day; every day, bang, bang, bang, just like that. So they sank another one on our land and then another one. Every single one of them produced oil. So that was it, there we were, we had a very big strike on our land.
LOUIE: We didn't think that it was going to go on much longer. Some lived like it *was* going to go on for ever. But we lived just like we'd always lived. Then one day the local newspaper printed a story about it. Letters started to come, cables, long distance phone calls, it was like suddenly everybody in the world knew about it and was begging us for our help.

Sad thing was you know, we reckoned some of the stories people told us about how much they needed money was true. But they just kept on and on coming, and how could you tell? Then one day someone said to us what we should do was think of something else instead to do with our money and throw all the letters in the fire. So that's what we did.

(It was Louie who decided what they could do with their money to help local people.)

LOUIE: "Harold," I said, "I've thought of an idea for something to do with our money, I've just been in the town to that old library, to get me a couple of books to read. You know what? I'm getting real tired of climbing up those library steps[2] every time I go there: it bothers my knees. So why don't we give the town a proper decent library where folk can walk right on in and choose a book for themselves without having to climb all those steps?"

(So Bird now has a new library, but Harold and Louie live in the same small house they've always lived in. Their lives haven't changed and neither have they.)

LOUIE: He's just exactly what he always was, ever since I've first knowed him: a sweet, nice, gentle man.

(from an article by Tony Parker in *The New Statesman*)

oil[1]: liquid found under the ground and used to make petrol for cars, fuel for
  planes etc.
steps[2]: you walk up steps to reach a door above the ground, to get onto a
  bus etc.

Which is the best summary?

A. Harold and Louie worked very hard in a shop until they were rich enough to buy an oil company. Lots of people asked them for money after that so they built a library. Apart from that their lives haven't changed.

B. Harold and Louie lived ordinary lives until an oil company found oil on their land. They became very rich and had lots of letters asking for money. They decided it was better to make their own decision, and so they built a new library. Apart from that their lives haven't changed.

C. Harold and Louie lived like ordinary people, working hard at their jobs. One day an oil company found oil on their land and they became very rich. They gave money to people who asked for it and paid for new steps for the library. Now they have an easy life and live in a big comfortable house.

Solutions to crosswords and problems

Revision Lesson A, Exercise 6

Lesson 7, Exercise 4

Spelling of regular past tenses
1. *Most regular verbs:*
   play + ed = played
2. *Verbs ending in -e:*
   hate + d = hated
3. *Short verbs ending in one vowel + one consonant:*
   shop + ped = shopped
4. *Verbs ending in consonant + y:*
   carry + ied = carried

Lesson 10, Exercise 3

The man in B has got longer hair. He is taller and thinner.

The woman in B has got bigger feet, she is a bit fatter, she has got shorter hair and a shorter skirt.

The picture is higher in B, the door is wider, and the room is lighter.

The cat is smaller in B.

Summary Lesson B, Exercise 6

Revision Lesson C, Exercise 6

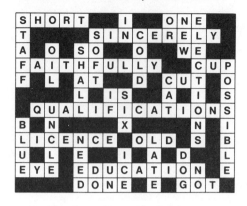

Revision Lesson D, Exercise 6

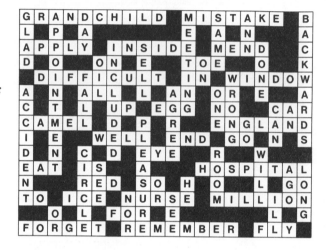

Lesson 26, Exercise 6

James won.

Lesson 27, Exercise 2

All the statements are true.

Revision Lesson E, Exercise 6

Lesson 34, Exercise 5

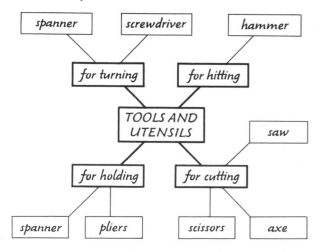

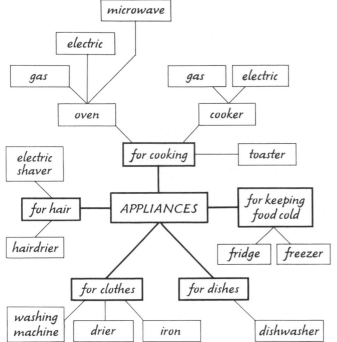

Lesson 35, Exercise 4

1. . . . or you can have three weeks in Cairo, return air fare, hotel room and full board, and a choice of excursions, for £1,500 inclusive.
2. What time is the next train to Godalming?
3. First on the right, second on the left. You can't miss it.
4. How long do you want to leave it for?
5. Do you mind if I open a window?
6. You go back down the road and stop the traffic. I'll phone for an ambulance.
7. 'How often are they supposed to run?'
   'Every ten minutes.'
   'The last one didn't stop, you know. It just went straight on.'
8. Have you got any hand baggage?
9. 'Do you know how fast you were going, sir?'
   'Er, about 40.'
   'You were doing 55, sir. Have you been drinking?'
10. Fill up with unleaded, please. And could you check the oil and the tyre pressures?
11. Hello, darling. I'm going to be a bit late, I'm afraid. There's a traffic jam a mile long.
12. We shall shortly be taking off on our flight to Rome. Please observe the no-smoking sign and ensure that your seat belt is fastened and your seat back is in the upright position.
13. Could you take me to Victoria, please?
14. It's making a funny noise, and it's very difficult to start from cold. And I think the brakes need checking. And it needs a service.

Revision Lesson F, Exercise 6

117

Acknowledgements

The authors and publishers are grateful to the following copyright owners for permission to reproduce photographs, illustrations, texts and music. Every endeavour has been made to contact copyright owners and apologies are expressed for any omissions.

page 7: *t* Extract from *Families and how to survive them* by Robin Skynner and John Cleese, by permission of Methuen London.   page 9: *tr* Extract from 'Honey Hunters of Nepal' by Eric Valli and Diane Summers, and *cr* photograph by Eric Valli, from *National Geographic* magazine, November 1988, courtesy of the National Geographic Society. page 10: *b* Reproduced by permission of *Punch*. page 14: Reprinted from WEEKEND Magazine.   page 15: *t* Extract from *The Martian Chronicles* by Ray Bradbury, published by Doubleday & Co. Inc. Reprinted by permission of Don Congdon Associates, Inc. Copyright © 1950, renewed 1977 by Ray Bradbury.   page 16: Reproduced by permission of *Punch*.   page 17: *cl* Reproduced by permission of Victorama Limited and S McMurtry; *cr* Reproduced by permission of *Punch*.   page 19: Reproduced by permission of *Punch*.   page 20: Cartoon by Heath reproduced by permission of the *Guardian*.   page 21: *bl* Reproduced by permission of *Punch*.   page 22: *tr* Courtesy of the *Oxford Mail*; *cl* Reproduced by permission of *Punch*.   page 24: Poem by Roland Tombekai Dempster from *Poems from Black Africa*, published by Indiana University Press; *c* Reproduced by permission of *Punch*.   page 25: Reproduced by permission of *Punch*.   page 26: Reproduced by permission of Harmsworth Publications Ltd.   page 28: *c* Text courtesy of Dick Francis and John Johnson (Authors' Agent) Limited; *b* Photograph courtesy of Clive Totman and the Barbican Centre, London.   page 31: *t* From the *Guinness Book of Records* © 1989 Guinness Publications Ltd by permission of Guinness Publishing Ltd.   page 32: Reproduced by permission of *Punch*. page 33: *bl* and *br* Reproduced by permission of *Punch*. page 35: *bl* and *br* Reproduced by permission of *Punch*. page 36: Copyright © 1956 by Ronald Searle from *Merry England* (Perpetua Books). Reprinted by permission of Tessa Sayle Agency.   page 38: *tl* Extract from *The Return of Heroic Failures* by Stephen Pile, copyright © Stephen Pile 1988. All rights reserved. Reproduced by kind permission of Martin Secker & Warburg and of Harper & Row Publishers, Inc.; *tr* © Mirror Group Newspapers.   page 41: *bl* and *br* Reprinted from WEEKEND Magazine.   page 44: *br* Reproduced by permission of *Punch*. page 45: Article reproduced by permission of Rex Features Ltd. page 46: Reproduced by permission of *Punch*. page 48: *br* © Mirror Group Newspapers.   page 50: Reprinted from WEEKEND Magazine.   page 51: *cl, bl* and *br* Reproduced by permission of *Punch*: *cr* Reprinted from WEEKEND Magazine.   page 53: Reproduced by permission of *Punch*. page 56: Reprinted from WEEKEND Magazine. page 58: *bl* Reproduced by permission of *Punch*: *br* © Mirror Group Newspapers.   page 60: *bl* Reproduced by permission of *Punch*: *br* © Express Newspapers plc.   page 61: *tr* Poem by Catherine Frankland from *Family and School*, Penguin Books Ltd; *b* Extract from *God Bless Love* compiled by Nanette Newman, reprinted by permission of Collins Publishers.   page 63: *cl, cr, bl* and *br* Reproduced by permission of *Punch*.   page 64. Reproduced by permission of *Punch*.   page 66: Reprinted from WEEKEND Magazine.   page 67: Text and illustration copyright © 1940 James Thurber. Copyright © 1968 Helen Thurber. From *Fables For Our Time*, published by Harper & Row, and *The Thurber Carnival* published by Hamish Hamilton Limited. By kind permission of Rosemary A Thurber.   page 68: *t* © Express Newspapers plc; *b* Roadsigns from *The Highway Code*, published by Her Majesty's Stationery Office, reproduced by kind permission of the Department of Transport.   page 69: *cr* Article reproduced from *The New Statesman* by permission of The New Statesman & Society; *bl* Reproduced by permission of *Punch*; *br* Reprinted from WEEKEND Magazine.   page 70: Text © Anna Tomforde.   page 72: *bl* Reprinted from WEEKEND Magazine: *br* Reproduced by permission of *Punch*.   page 74: Reproduced by permission of *Punch*.   page 75: *t, bl* and *br* Reproduced by permission of *Punch*.   page 76: *cr* Poem by Bob Rogers, reprinted by kind permission of the author: *b* Reproduced by permission of *Punch*.   page 77: *bl* Reprinted from WEEKEND Magazine; *br* © Mirror Group Newspapers.   page 108 *t* Poem 'Chant' from the Dinka people of the Sudan. Reprinted by permission of Faber and Faber Ltd from *Voices from Twentieth-Century Africa*, collected by Chinweizu; *b* Adapted from an article by John Bailey in *Forward*, June 1989, text and photograph by kind permission of the Guide Dogs for the Blind Association.   page 109:

l Adapted from an article in YOU Magazine. Text and photograph by permission of Solo Syndication & Literary Agency Ltd; *r* Extract from *Vital Statistics* by Gyles Brandreth © Gyles Brandreth.   page 110: *l* Text adapted from an article in COMPANY Magazine by permission of the National Magazine Company Ltd; photograph by Jeremy Pembrey; *r* Adapted from 'Talk', a story told by the Ashanti people of Ghana. Reprinted by permission of Faber and Faber Ltd from *Voices from Twentieth-Century Africa*, collected by Chinweizu. page 111: *l* Adapted from an article in *Best*, by kind permission of *Best* Magazine; *r* Extract by kind permission of A P Watt Ltd on behalf of Ved Mehta. page 112:   *tl* Article originally entitled 'Labrador crash pilot versus the elements' © The Daily Telegraph plc; *bl* Adapted from *Going Solo* by Roald Dahl, published by Jonathan Cape Ltd and Penguin Books Ltd. Copyright © 1987 by Roald Dahl. Reprinted by permission of Farrar, Straus and Giroux, Inc. Photograph from Bruce Colman Limited.   page 113: *l* Adapted from an article in the *Guardian*, 22 October 1989, by Victor Keegan, photograph by Graham Turner, used by permission of the *Guardian*; *r* Adapted from 'For Poorer, For Richer' by Tony Parker, copyright © 1989 by Tony Parker. First appeared in *The New Statesman*, adapted by Tony Parker from *A Place Called Bird* published by Secker & Warburg.

The authors and publishers are grateful to the following:

Young Artists: Sarah John, pages 15 *b* and 58 *cr*. Amy Burch, pages 57 and 62.

Maggie Mundy: Ann Johns, pages 10 *tr* and 11. Hemesh Alles, pages 21 *tr*, 28 *cr*, 29 and 42. Sharron Pallent, pages 30, 31 *b*, 48 *bl* and 49.

Artists Partners: Derek Brazell, pages 9 *bl* and *br*, 13, 27, 37, 47, 73 *t* and *br*.

The Inkshed: Julia Bigg, page 34.

Stephen Conlin, pages 7 *bl*, 54 and 65.   Tony Richards, pages 40 and 76 *t*.   Nancy Anderson, page 44 *c*. Lester Meacham, pages 70 and 71.

t = top   *b* = bottom   *c* = centre   *r* = right   *l* = left

cool — преврат
to decide
expel — изхвърлям
deadline — срок (dedlain)

their defence
abuse of power — злоупотреб
с власт